PUBLISHED BY BOOM BOOKS

www.boombooks.biz

ABOUT THIS SERIES

.... But after that, I realised that I knew very little about these parents of mine. They had been born about the start of the Twentieth Century, and they died in 1970 and 1980. For their last 50 years, I was old enough to speak with a bit of sense.

I could have talked to them a lot about their lives. I could have found out about the times they lived in. But I did not. I know almost nothing about them really. Their courtship? Working in the pits? The Lock-out in the Depression? Losing their second child? Being dusted as a miner? The shootings at Rothbury? My uncles killed in the War? Love on the dole? There were hundreds, thousands of questions that I would now like to ask them. But, alas, I can't. It's too late.

Thus, prompted by my guilt, I resolved to write these books. They describe happenings that affected people, real people. The whole series is, to coin a modern phrase, designed to push your buttons, to make you remember and wonder at things forgotten.

The books might just let nostalgia see the light of day, so that oldies and youngies will talk about the past and re-discover a heritage otherwise forgotten. Hopefully, they will spark discussions between generations, and foster the asking and answering of questions that should not remain unanswered.

ABOUT THIS BOOK

I was born in 1934, so that I can remember well a great deal of what went on around me from 1939 onwards. But of course, the bulk of this book's material came from research. That meant that I spent many hours in front of a computer reading electronic versions of newspapers, magazines, Hansard, Ministers' Press releases and the like. My task was to sift out, day-by-day, those stories and events that would be of interest to the most readers.

Then I supplemented these with materials from books, broadcasts, memoirs, biographies, government reports and statistics. And I talked to old-timers, one-on-one, and in organised groups, and to Baby Boomers about their recollections. People with stories to tell came out of the woodwork, and talked no end about the tragic, and funny, and commonplace events that have shaped their lives.

I think I have covered most of the major issues that people then were interested in. On the other hand, in some cases I have dwelt a little on minor frivolous matters, perhaps to the detriment of more sober considerations. Still, in the long run, this makes the book more readable, and hopefully it will convey adequately the spirit of the times.

Overall, I expect I can make you wonder, remember, rage and giggle, and I hope that you and your family will find some comfort in the realisation that no matter how new and novel a current situation is to you, it has all happened often before.

BORN IN 1960?
WHAT ELSE HAPPENED?

RON WILLIAMS

AUSTRALIAN SOCIAL HISTORY

BOOK 22 IN A SERIES OF 34
FROM 1939 to 1972

War Babies Years (1939 to 1945):   7 Titles
Baby Boom Years (1946 to 1960):   15 Titles
Post Boom Years (1961 to 1972):   12 Titles

BOOM, BOOM BABY, BOOM

BORN IN 1960? WHAT ELSE HAPPENED?

Published by Boom Books
Wickham, NSW, Australia
Web: www.boombooks.biz
Email: email@boombooks.biz

© Ron Williams 2013. This edition 2021

Creator: Williams, Ron, 1934- author.

Title: Born in 1960? : what else happened?

ISBN: 9780648771678

Subjects:Australia--History--Miscellanea--20th century.

Cover images: National Archives of Australia:

A1200 11873065, schoolboy

A1200 11657907, holiday fashions

A1200 11303535, Melbourne Cup fashions

A1200 11404490, children at a music class

CONTENTS

OUR WOMEN ARE DRUNKS   1

HOSPITAL MATTERS   10

VICE-REGAL AND REGAL   11

FRUIT BARROWS IN THE CITY   20

NOT AT ALL POST HASTE   23

BIG TROUBLE IN SOUTH AFRICA   30

APRIL FOOLS' DAY?   37

NSW HOSPITALS.   39

GARY POWERS AND THE SPY- PLANE   55

TWO MURDERS IN MAITLAND   60

BABES IN DAD'S ARMS   69

WHITE VERSUS BLACK? COMING TO YOU?   74

GRAEME THORNE KIDNAPPED   83

WHAT'S HAPPENING TO MIGRANTS?   89

GRAEME THORNE'S BODY FOUND   97

LIQUOR FOR ABORIGINES   101

MAX GLUCKMAN   113

BENEFITS FOR EX-SERVICEMEN   120

THE GREATEST SHOW ON EARTH   129

THE RABBIT MENACE   136

TOUGH TIMES NOW CLOSER?   139

OUR CENSORS ON THE BALL   142

CHRISTMAS - AGAIN   153

GRAEME THORNE INQUEST   155

SUMMING UP   163

PEOPLE AND RECORDS

Australian Prime Minister	Bob Menzies
Opposition Leader	Doc Evatt
Governor General	Viscount Dunrossil
British Monarch	Queen Elizabeth
British Prime Minister	Harold McMillan
British Opposition	Churchill
The Pope	John XXIII
US President	Eisenhower
Leader of the Badies	Khrushchev
Australian cricket captain	Richard Benaud

MELBOURNE CUP

1959	Macdougall
1960	Hi Jinx
1961	Lord Fury

THE ASHES

1958 - 59	Australia 4 - 1
1961	Drawn 2 - 2
1962 - 63	England 3 - 1

INTRODUCTION

This book is the 22nd in a series of books that I have researched and written. It tells a story about a number of important or newsworthy Australia-centric events that happened in 1960. The series covers each of the years from 1939 to 1972 for a total of 34 books.

I developed my interest in writing thesebooks a few years ago at a time when my children entered their teens. My own teens started in 1947, and I started trying to remember what had happened to me then. I thought of the big events first, like Saturday afternoon at the pictures, and cricket in the back yard, and the wonderful fun of going to Maitland on the train for school each day. Then I recalled some of the not-so-good things. I was an altar boy, and that meant three or four Masses a week. I might have thought I loved God at that stage, but I really hated his Masses. And the schoolboy bullies, like Greg Favvell, and the hapless Freddie Ebans. Yet, to compensate for these, there was always the beautiful, black headed, blue-sailor-suited June Brown, who I was allowed to worship from a distance.

I also thought about my parents. Most of the major events that I lived through came to mind readily. But after that, I realised that I really knew very little about these parents of mine. They had been born about the start of the Twentieth Century, and they died in 1970 and 1980. For their last 20 years, I was old enough to speak with a bit of sense. I could have talked to them a lot about their lives. I could have found out about the times they lived in. But I did not. I know almost nothing about them really. Their courtship? Working in the pits? The Lock-out in the Depression?

Losing their second child? Being dusted as a miner? The shootings at Rothbury? My uncles killed in the War? There were hundreds, thousands of questions that I would now like to ask them. But, alas, I can't. It's too late.

Thus, prompted by my guilt, I resolved to write these books. They describe happenings that affected people, real people. In 1960, there is some coverage of international affairs, but a lot more on social events within Australia. This book, and the whole series is, to coin a modern phrase, designed to push the reader's buttons, to make you remember and wonder at things forgotten. The books might just let nostalgia see the light of day, so that oldies and youngies will talk about the past and re-discover a heritage otherwise forgotten. Hopefully, they will spark discussions between generations, and foster the asking and the answering of questions that should not remain unanswered.

The sources of my material. I was born in 1934, so that I can remember well a great deal of what went on around me from 1939 onwards. But of course, the bulk of this book's material came from research. That meant that I spent many hours in front of a computer reading electronic versions of newspapers, magazines, Hansard, Ministers' Press releases and the like. My task was to sift out, day-by-day, those stories and events that would be of interest to the most readers. Then I supplemented these with materials from books, broadcasts, memoirs, biographies, government reports and statistics. And I talked to old-timers, one-on-one, and in organised groups, and to Baby Boomers about their recollections. People with stories to tell came out of the woodwork, and talked no end about the tragic, and funny, and commonplace events that have shaped their very different lives.

The presentation of each book. For each year covered, the end result is a collection of short Chapters on many of the topics that concerned ordinary people in that year. I think I have covered most of the major issues that people then were interested in. On the other hand, in some cases I have dwelt a little on minor frivolous matters, perhaps to the detriment of more sober considerations. Still, in the long run, this makes the book more readable, and hopefully it will convey adequately the spirit of the times.

Each of the books is mainly Sydney based, but I have been deliberately national in outlook, so that readers elsewhere will feel comfortable that I am talking about matters that affected them personally. After all, housing shortages and strikes and juvenile delinquency involved all Australians, and other issues, such as problems overseas, had no State component in them. **Overall, I expect I can make you wonder, remember, rage and giggle equally, no matter where you hail from.**

BACKGROUND FROM 1959

The year 1959 had ended on a good note for the 10 million Australians living and working and playing here. In general, everyone who wanted a job could get one, most people could afford a TV set, and live in a decent house, half of them had cars, and there was plenty of food and drink for their tables. People were healthy by the world standard of that time, and indeed, life expectancy was starting to rise at a good rate. This was not a rich economy, but at least what wealth there was here was spread more or less evenly though the community, so that real suffering was about as small as you can get in a society like ours.

The New Year came in without the usual bang. The newspapers across the nation said that it was the quietest beginning for decades, and even the number of well-meaning patronising old fogies who usually gave us messages of hope (mingled with exhortations to work harder), was down. **Bob Menzies**, who was still Prime Minister of Australia after 10 years in office, and not to be described as an old fogie, was of the opinion that "Our country was built on work, skill and friendliness. We have immeasurable talent for these three great gifts, and as long as we use them to our fullest extent, our future will be secure. We must never forget that there is no substitute for hard work and true enterprise."

The Leader of the Opposition, Dr Evatt, who had also held that position for about as long as Menzies, said that the Great Powers, Russia and America, had shown sincerity in their mutual discussions, and it was to be hoped that they could settle their differences without recourse to war. Both of these were good, true and heartening messages, and were welcome, but I suspect that most people were more interested in how they would be spending their month of lassitude and frivolity that always came with the New Year.

INTERNATIONAL SITUATION

Evatt's message, however, served as a reminder that, despite the silver lining that he saw right now, the two major blocs of the world were caught up in the vast ideological battle called the Cold War. This pointless exercise had been going on for a decade, and would in fact go on for quite a few decades more.

The way it worked was that **Russia and America** each wanted world control, that some people called hegemony. So they were busy trying to get all the nations of the world to join either the Communist camp, or the Capitalist establishment. **To gain this support from these nations, they cajoled, bullied, bribed, deceived, and you-name-it at all times.** This meant that each of them was involved in fighting little wars on foreign shores, as patriots if you were on their side, or as terrorists if you were not. And each of them had the great intellectual and ideological weapons behind them in that they had atom bombs of ridiculous power so that they could threaten any nation or the world with destruction if things did not work out their way.

The posturing and bickering and Machiavellian betrayal and shenanigans had been going on for ten years, and the Australian population were not interested in them any more. The newspapers and politicians kept up a barrage of propaganda telling us how bad the Russians were and the Russians in turn, did the same at home and with **their** allies. But Dr Evatt's statement that the Great Powers were getting on well was buried in a small paragraph in Page Four of the newspapers, and was forgotten as soon as it was read.

But having dismissed the Cold War at the start of 1960 so easily, let me add two riders. **First**, not everyone was as unconcerned as I was. A number of people, particularly teenagers perhaps, **were** concerned by the thought that tonight a nuclear bomb would wipe out their city, and they **did** live in the shadow of the bomb. I think, though, that such people were few and far between.

Second, the spiel about the War and the Bomb and the Communists was everywhere. Just about e**very newspaper**, **every day**, carried some reference to the menaces facing us through the war, on **every one of their first five pages**. The build-up was non-stop, all pervasive. Having said that, I will not burden you with this propaganda throughout this book, and will instead refer to it only where I know it might have some consequence. Remember though, every now and then, that it is always in the air.

One little war that **does** deserve comment now is **the conflict brewing in Algeria**. This nation, just south of Spain, across the Straits of Gibraltar near the entrance to the Mediterranean Sea, was currently under French control, and its population was made up of millions of Muslims, mainly of Arab stock, and less than one million French settlers. The French Government, under Prime Minister General de Gaulle, had decided that the nation should become independent of France, and be given the right to self-determination.

However, the French settlers saw that if that happened, they would be very much in the minority, and thought that the favoured positions that they currently occupied would be denied them. Thus, at the start on 1960, they were offering serious military resistance to the French authorities there, even to the point of having some minor military scuffles with them A small, but growing number of lives was being lost in these little battles between French soldiers on the one hand, and French settlers on the other. This is a situation that will develop, and I will return to it as the months pass.

THE TRIAL OF MAX STUART

This trial had been controversial, and it was especially so in his home State of South Australia.

Stuart, an Aboriginal, had been charged with the murder of a 13-year old girl at Ceduna. He had been found guilty, and been sentenced to death. He lost several appeals, including one to the Privy Council in England, but there was doubt over the validity of his confession, so a Royal Commission was set up to look into the matter. The Commission found that the verdict of guilty should stand, but in the meantime, because of the length of time the various legal proceedings had taken, his death sentence was reduced to life imprisonment.

Rupert Murdoch was a newspaper proprieter in Adelaide at the time, and he strongly advocated for Stuart. He had an offsider, the now-famous Rohan Rivett. After the Commission made its decision, the State Government started proceedings against their paper and Rivett, and again, as the months pass, we will return to the events as they unfold.

A FINAL LOOK AT THE FIFTIES

Before we get into the hurly burley of the Sixties, we should look back to note a few changes that had happened since **1950**. I will limit myself to four such changes.

First change. War-time rationing **then** was imposed on items such as petrol, tea, butter, gas and electricity. Beer had been hard to get, and bottled beer was a luxury, especially around Christmas. There were very few wine drinkers in this bronzed nation, and whisky and other spirits were not on the menu. Tobacco as such was virtually rationed, and you needed to be an ex-Serviceman to get a regular quota of cigarettes.

By 1960, such restrictions were just matters of history.

Second change. Hire Purchase had come, and television came at about the same time. Over the decade, it became possible to buy electrical goods, and cars, **on the never-never**, and everyone did that. Compared to 1950, cars now were everywhere, roads were crowded, parking machines were taking over the cities, the tow-truck industry was making its dubious living, and Public Transport was getting further and further behind. The palliative for this was TV. Just about every home had a set now in the lounge, where Bob Dyer and, until recently, Jack Davey were also regular guests.

Third change. The Baby Boom had arrived. In 1950, the war was long since over, and people had slowly adjusted to that. The melancholy and worry that had marked the War-years was giving way to a lighter attitude to life, but it had no real focus for a few years. But when the Baby Boom got under way, this is what the nation focussed on. Courtship and marriage, having children, getting finance and then a house, and a car, and a Victor mower, and a Hills Hoist, all of these became the staff of life. By 1960, this attitude of adventure within respectability still dominated, so this book is off to a good start.

Fourth change. Back in 1950, we had never heard of bodgies, Argentine Ants, Golden Staph, or Rock 'n' Roll. We had no non-iron shirts, espresso bars, or plastic paint. Hotels closed at 6 p.m., and the door-to-door salesman was still welcome. How, I ask, could anyone survive under such primitive conditions?

MY RULES IN WRITING

Before we plunge into 1960, I will explain to you a few of the standards I stick to in writing.

NOTE. Throughout this book, I rely a lot on re-producing Letters from the newspapers. Whenever I do this, I put the text in a different font, and indent it a little, and make the font somewhat smaller. **I do not edit the text at all**. That is, I do not correct spelling or grammar, and if the text gets at all garbled, I do not change it. It's just as it was seen in the Papers.

SECOND NOTE. The material for this book that comes from newspapers is reported as it was seen at the time. If the benefit of hindsight over the years changes things, then I **might** record that in my **Comments**. The info reported thus reflects matters **as they were read in 1960.**

THIRD NOTE. Let me also apologise in advance to anyone I might offend. In a work such as this, it is certain some people will think I got some things wrong. I am sure that I did, but please remember, all of this is **only my opinion**. And really, **my opinion does not matter one little bit in the scheme of things. I hope you will say "silly old bugger", shrug your shoulders, and read on.**

BUT FIRST, A LETTER FROM 1950

In 1960, I had moved out of the family nest, and was roosting in the Big Smoke in Sydney. My father and I wrote weekly, and at the turn of the decade he asked me to pick out one change I had noticed since 1950.

I enclose part of my response. "People are ever so more confident. The hesitaions that were apparent a decade ago have gone. They are no longer remembering the shadows of the War, and the restrictions and the rules and the rationing.

"They are not worried about housing, nor about the threats of the clergy, about poverty and their jobs. They **know** that if bad things happen, they can cope, and the solemn dread of the pre-war years just does not make them fearful any more. They are now a nation of doers, not a fearful nation or worriers."

JANUARY NEWS : OUR WOMEN ARE DRUNKS

Dr Andrew Ivy, an American, was visiting Sydney to give a series of lectures on the evils of alcoholic drink. He was President of the International Commission for the Prevention of Alcoholism, and was scheduled to give a series of lectures at the University of Sydney's Great Hall in the next week.

Yesterday, he made two comments that raised the ire of doctors, psychiatrists, social workers, and research workers. The first such statement was that he had no interest in a cure for alcoholism, because it was incurable. This of course dismayed all of the above experts, because it seemed to say that their combined efforts were useless. In fact, though, his attention-getting statement would have passed mainly unnoticed, but for what he followed up with.

He went on to say that there was a larger percentage of women drinkers in Australia than in America, and that he had not seen so many drunken women on the streets since London in 1925.

There weren't too many experts available here to make a good comparison with London in 1925, but a lot were prepared to take this gentleman to task over our level of drunkenness. Needless to say all the above professional groups sprang to the defence of Australian womanhood.

For example, Dr Yeomans, from the North Ryde Alcoholic Clinic, said "it is difficult to believe that Dr Ivy found 50 women staggering drunk, as he claimed, in King's Cross." Then there was the argument from Mr O Williams of the Foundation for Research and Treatment of Alcoholism. He defended our women – at least, I think it was a defence – by saying "Australian women alcoholics tend to be wardrobe drinkers. They rarely appear drunk in public."

Letters, Al Coholic, Broughton Hall. Mr Ivy has got it all wrong. I am committed to this institution because of alcohol has ruined my life. I do not agree that there is no cure for alcoholism, because I have seen first hand that cures do work. I am much better under the care here than I have been for 10 years.

But to get to the serious claim he made that Australian women were drunks. Where are they then? They are not here. If they are drunks, where do they all go? There is not one in this institution. There should be. Think of what parties we could have if we got together expert drinkers of both sexes in a never-ending party, and were waited on hand-and-foot like we are here now. Don't tell me we can't get alcohol. We can always get alcohol. What we need is the women.

NEWS LIBEL CASE

Abridged Press report. *News Limited,* an Adelaide newspaper owned by Rupert Murdoch, was issued with summonses charging that it had published libels during the Stuart Royal Commission late last year. They were issued by the South Australian Police on behalf of the Crown. The maximum penalty was a fine of one thousand Pounds, or one year's imprisonment, or both, on each charge. In all, a fine of nine thousand Pounds was possible.

The summonses alleged that the following headlines or posters were published during the trial:

SHAND BLASTS NAPIER

SHAND QUITS. YOU WON'T GIVE US A FAIR GO

THESE MEN CAN'T DO THE JOB: SHAND

Napier was one of the three Commissioners. Shand was the most-respected QC who was appearing for Stuart. Sadly, he died before the Commission brought down his judgement.

The summonses **charged the defendants with having published these libels, knowing them to be false.** They would be heard first in the Adelaide Police Court, and then they might go on to a Supreme Court Judge and jury.

Adelaide, January 25, Press report. Mr J Travers, acting for the South Australian Crown, opening the trial said that News had sought to bring the Royal Commission into malice, hatred and disrespect,

These facts disclose a singularly serious offence in this case because they strike a blow at the judiciary and the judges. **They are designed to stir up mass distrust and hysteria.** The easiest and surest way of undermining the stability of any country is to shake the confidence of the people in the judiciary.

January 26. Travers said that Shand had made none of the comments attributed to him. He went on to say "These placards indicate the malice and hatred and contempt into which they are seeking to bring the judges. The posters are the product of a mind either diseased or distorted with malice."

January 29. Rupert Murdoch was called in evidence, but refused to say whether he had any part in deciding what the headlines were to be on that day. He refused to answer on the grounds that his answers might be used to incriminate him.

After three and a half days of hearing, the Court found that News and Rivett both had a case to answer, and committed Rivett for trail. Such an event would not come before the Supreme Court before March.

Comment. The very emotional and un-legal language used by Mr Travers indicate how strongly the Crown and the Government felt abut this matter. It will be interesting to come back to it in later months.

AMERICAN POLITICS

This was an election year in America. Candidates were starting to get themselves ready for their primaries, and were playing all sorts of coy games about whether they would stand or not. This year, the Democrats were unusually quick off the mark and Hubert Humphrey had already said he was a definite starter.

Press report. Now a relative unknown has stepped up, and said he too would stand. **His name is John Kennedy, aged 42, and a Senator from Massachusetts.** It is well known that Kennedy is a practising Catholic, so there is considerable doubt about whether he will poll well.

As for the Republicans, only one candidate has so far nominated. **That is the** existing Vice-President, Richard Nixon. At the moment, he is playing second fiddle to President Eisenhower, but his stocks have risen recently because of his part in settling the steel dispute, and it could be that he could be seen as suited for the higher mantle.

RE-GROWTH OF THE NAZI PARTY

Authorities in Germany have become alarmed over the recent desecration of a Jewish synagogue, and other anti-Semitic acts throughout the nation.

News report, Berlin. There is a widespread and secret fear among German middle-class and conservatives that the ghost of Hitler is still haunting the country. For these people, this fear is never spoken about, the events of the Hitler years are never discussed, the history of the war-years is better forgotten. But recent attacks on synagogues are forcing public debate on all matters relating to the Hitler regime. Of particular interest is the number of youths who are turning to pro-Nazi groups, and the likelihood that they will become anti-social or violent.

There are a number of youth groups with openly Nazi names, such as "Viking Youth", "Young Steel Helmets", and the propaganda brochures they read are typically titled "The Storm City". A survey done by German Trade Unions said recently that about 50,000 youths were now members of such groups , and believes that there is a co-ordinating link between the various individual cells.

This outbreak of anti-Semitic pro-Nazi activity in Cologne unleashed similar defacements of synagogues in London, Lisbon, Cyprus, South Africa, the United States, Austria and

France. In all of these cities, large public demonstrations were in turn held protesting against the daubings.

Sydney observers also were alarmed.

Letter, Professor H Cowan. The short statement of the German Embassy in Canberra in your recent issue sounds regrettably like those put out by the German diplomatic mission in the years preceding and following Hitler's accession to power. I remember only too clearly how anti-Semitic excesses were all blamed on a small subnormal minority; yet this minority succeeded in gaining power and murdering millions of Jews. Mention of this fact today produces only an embarrassed silence.

Unfortunately, a whole generation, now approaching middle age, has been indoctrinated by the Nazi regime, and it is among these people, rather than the Nazi Old Guard, that a new Fascist movement is likely to form.

Letters, Dr S Goldberg. Among the many reactions which the recent world-wide acts of anti-Semitism have evoked, the absence of apathy which characterised the onset of Hitler's regime gives one hope that this world of ours is really undergoing a change of heart.

During the decade before the War, we only heard half-hearted protests against the atrocities. Now we see a revulsion and determination to stamp out the plague of racial discrimination.

Letters, A Shephard. Anti-Semitism is only one of the bad aspects of Nazism. Let us not forget that, according to the prosecutors at Nuremburg, 12 million people were murdered by the Naxis. Only half of these were Jews. The resurgence of Nazism is not merely a Jewish matter. It is much more the concern of Gentiles.

Comment. Despite the bristling of the world against these anti-Semitic and pro-Nazi acts, they still continued throughout the year, in Germany and elsewhere, and have continued off and on right up to the present day.

MEMORIES OF AN OZ PIONEER

Letters, Frank O'Grady. If one is accustomed to travel the road between Sydney and Melbourne which follows the route taken the explorer, the name of Hamilton Hume is constantly brought to mind. The Hume Highway, the Hume Dam, sundry Hume hotels, and commercials help to perpetrate the memory of Australia's first native-born explorer.

Yet the home that he built for himself and Elizabeth Dight, on the sunlit plains of Yass, decays on the hillside near the Canberra turn-off without even a notice-board to enlighten the traveller. For ordinary Australians, Cooma Cottage means nothing.

The tree under which the explorer rested in 1821 leans gnarled and seared beside the old colonial mansion. The spacious entrance hall houses a farm tractor. While the bronze weathercock turns in the wind on the roof of the stables, turkeys inhabit the outhouses. The visitor has a mid-Victorian spaciousness, of cracked wall, of shingled roof beneath rusted sheets of imported English flat iron. And Jack Burke, resident owner for the past 36 years, brings out for signature a school exercise book with a brief but faithful history handwritten over the first four pages.

There one sees the autographs of the few who know that this was the last home of the Davy Crockett of Australia – the lad who discovered the Wingecarribbee at the age of 17, who opened up a road from Sydney to Jervis Bay, discovered the Goulbourn Plains, the Murrumbidgee country, and, while still little more than a boy, **found the Murray River** and opened up the country from the Murrumbidgee to Port Phillip.

How can any Australian allow the home of our greatest early-nineteenth-century national to fall into ruin for the lack of a few Pounds and the will to preserve it? In any other country but this, Cooma Cottage would be a national memorial.

Letter, Stuart Hume, Garroorigang, Goulbourn. I have known Cooma Cottage and its present owner, Jack Borke, for over 40 years, and its condition has altered little during that time. It would cost more than a few Pounds to restore it.

If I remember correctly, one of the first to suggest the idea of a national memorial was Mr Justice Ferguson, then a circuit judge, and author. You would have little chance of assembling any of the explorer's personal effects. They were dispersed far and wide when he died. A grazier near Gunning has his double bed. A confectioner at Young boasted his brolly. His grandfather clock is in a second-hand shop in Sydney's Neutral Bay.

The last I heard (about 1934) and on surprisingly good authority, was that a well-known medico was hawking the explorer's gold watch around Sydney, trying to sell it for fifty Pounds......

McAlister, a business associate of Hume, described him as a massive man with a direct manner. He had that all right, and it is sad to see Cooma as it is, for he liked everything to be right up to the knocker, even dress when it adorned his relatives.

My grandfather once took my grandmother to dine with the explorer at Cooma. Gran, though an astute woman, had little dress sense, but she did her best for the occasion. Hamilton greeted them civilly enough then turned to grandfather and exploded "My God, Andrew, Can't you afford to dress the woman better that that?" He became very irascible in his old age.

However, if you feel like a fishing trip, and visit Cooma, you will get a better reception now. Jack will be glad to see you, and if you happen to have a bit of the past in your pocket, you'll be right for a cup of tea.

I'll be surprised if the sun will ever rise again on old Cooma as it was in his heyday, but of one thing I am certain. If the old man was to return tomorrow, he'd stir the possum in some one.

Comment. The Cooma homestead was resurrected, by the National Trust in 1971.

HOSPITAL MATTERS

The Secretary of the NSW Hospitals' Association today made **a plea for more male nurses** for the State. He said that female nurses were leaving in droves and the ideal solution would be for the recruitment of more male nurses. Prejudices against male nurses were psychological. "Trained Australian male nurses go to England and are absorbed easily there, but there's nothing for them here. One of four nurses in England are male."

Contact with patients. Matron Edna Parmeter, from Cronulla, in a letter to the Herald wrote "It is only right and proper that migrants to a country should realise that their first duty is to learn the language, and that hospital staff should not be expected to provide assistance here." This was in answer to a Letter that suggested it would be helpful if a smattering of Italian language was introduced into the training of nurses.

The Matron went of to say "**In any case, we matrons do not encourage chatter between nurse and patient.**"

Comment. This dear matron did not win many friends with these statements. It was a time when Matrons were under wide attack for their toughness, and for the fact that their impersonal approach flowed right down the chain to the detriment of patients.

FEBRUARY: VICE-REGAL AND REGAL

Lord Dunrossil arrived by air in Australia on February 1st, and after giving the nation a brief once-over, decided he would like to work here. The Prime Minister, Bob Menzies, who happened to be at the airport, suggested that there was a vacancy here for a Governor General. Dunrossil hardly gave it a thought, and accepted on the spot. They agreed that he should take up the position on the next day, with scarcely enough time to fill in all the required paper-work needed for the Public Service, and getting a security clearance.

Meanwhile, Lady Dunrossil was waiting inside the terminal. She was told of the decision and was delighted. As it turned out, both of these gentle-folk were particularly well suited for his job, and it was with great sadness that the nation heard of his death about a year later.

Another Royal mouth to feed. Bob Menzies somehow worked out early in February that Queen Elizabeth was intending to have another baby towards the end of the month. He, of course, could not contain himself, and blabbed this information to an unsuspecting but delighted world forthwith. In fact, he went further, he actually made an appeal to the Australian public to make the announcement of the birth a "most memorable occasion." He called for every private citizen, and organisations with a flag to "fly it on this great occasion".

He indicated that salutes of 21 guns would fire salvos, RAAF planes would fly over every capital city, and the Royal Australian Navy would dress its ships. He made his announcement on February 10th, and this got the nation all excited.

But we all had to wait breathless for 10 more days, until the blessed event **did** happen. A small boy arrived, he was well and the Queen was well. And Menzies' festivities **did** happen, even the bells at St Mark's in Sydney's Darling Point rang out for 15 minutes from 2.45 a.m. Congratulations and good wishes flooded the Queen and family from right across the Commonwealth, and the occasion was most joyous indeed.

In a more staid London, several lucky people actually got tangible rewards. The Welsh Guards, who were on duty at Buckingham Palace when the baby was born, got a traditional bounty to celebrate the occasion. Two sergeants received seven shillings each, two corporals got four shillings, and 20 guardsmen gleaned one shilling and sixpence each.

Whither Princess Margaret? Margaret was Elizabeth's sister. The heir to the throne was Prince Charles, and Margaret had been second in line. Now that another male was on the scene, Margaret dropped down a notch.

But, coincidentally, she had other things to think about. Just about a week after the royal birth, it was announced that **Margaret was to marry Anthony Armstrong-Jones,** a fine young photographer of the London social scene. He was reported to be affable and gregarious with a liking for beer and jazz. "He is slim and good-looking, and is a few months older than Margaret, and a few inches taller. The couple will marry in June, and at that time her

State allowance will increase from 6,000 Pounds a year to 15,000 Pounds. Though it should be noted that she has other endowments from her Grandmother and other relatives. There is some early speculation as to whether he will be given a title, but in view of lack of precedent, it is too early to say."

"Armstrong-Jones is an old Etonian. At the age of 11, he was put of action with polio, and it was during his period of immobilisation that he developed his interest in photography. As a young man he wrote to the Duchess of Kent, and asked if he could take the official photographs for the 21st birthday of the Duke of Kent. Given that the Duke was also an old Etonian, Jones got the job. From there, his reputation as a social photographer was assured. Probably his most famous subject, apart from the Royal family, was Paul Robeson, the American negro bass, when he was starring as Othello in King Lear at Stratford-on-Avon."

Comment. The interest in all these regal events was very large and genuine. People from all walks of life were still interested in the British Royals, and it is interesting to note that, for this month, the nascent but quickly-growing obsession with American Hollywood stars and US entertainers was kept right out of the Press.

JACK KRAMER AND HIS TROUPE

Jack Kramer was born in 1921 in Las Vegas, Nevada. He came to prominence in tennis in the 1940's, playing and winning in large American tournaments, and representing America in the Davis Cup. Tennis in those days was completely amateur, but about 1950 this thoroughly-likable man left the hallowed ranks of amateurs and formed his own troupe of professionals.

Up till now, champions like Sedgeman and McGregor, had held down jobs during the day, and played tennis in the evenings and at the weekend. If they won tournaments, they could keep some of the money, and if they represented Australia, they were paid a stipend and an allowance. But the payment from "Tennis Australia" was meagre. So the idea of a professional group of players, who were always paid, and who were fulltime tennis pros, was a very different one indeed.

Hostility to these new performers was very great. For example, Australian tennis bodies said that their players were banned from playing against the pros, and the courts that they used were not available for the interlopers. Nevertheless, Kramer kept touring the world, with a group of more-or-less permanent persons travelling with him, competing with themselves and natives from the countries he visited. Kramer's troupe became popular watching in many capitals cities of the world.

But times were changing in sport. *Professionalism* was growing in cricket, fees for Rugby players were being slowly increased, and players could only stay on top if they practised more and moved towards full-time "work" in their chosen sport.

By 1960, for ten years, the amateurs and the pros had been battling for supremacy. The amateurs objected to the pros because **they put nothing back into the game**. They took their money and went. The amateur bodies supported facilities right round the country, and ran coaching classes and tournaments for tens of thousands of juniors round the nation.

So, in 1960, the Australian Lawn Tennis Association met to discuss the staging of **open** tennis tournaments, where amateurs and pros competed on equal terms. In the course of these discussions, the various States had their say. Many State delegates did not like the Kramer way of tennis.

Victoria said that Kramer was on the way out, and now was the time to kick him. Queensland thought that if the amateurs played the pros, the pros would be completely rubbed out. NSW warned it was violently opposed to open tennis. It considered that, while Kramer was a charming fellow, he was interested only in the money, and he had not helped out thousands and thousands of juniors one bit. It added that Dwight Davis would turn in his grave if pros ever played in the Davis Cup. Tasmania was different. It asserted that our amateurs were no longer fully amateur, and that the game was not played for the old-fashioned ideal of love of the game.

When a vote was taken, three States were opposed to open tennis, and three States were for it. The Chairman voted **for** expansion to allow pros to participate. England and the US had already agreed to **one** tournament each year being played on an open basis, and Australia now similarly decided that the next Australian Championships should conform to the new pattern. The end of an era was nigh; tennis was no longer a gentlemen's sport. It was to become a commercial enterprise.

Comment. After the War, in 1946, I can remember the English cricket team coming onto and off the field at the Sydney Cricket Ground. The few pros came from one entrance, and the amateurs came from another. The two groups were part of the same team, yet they had separate dressing rooms and entrances.

A few years later, about 1954, Sedgeman and McGregor gave an exhibition game or two on the grass courts at Sydney University. They were approached after the play had finished and asked if they wanted payment. They each asked for their bus and train fare, and for the value of their sandwich lunch. Needless to say, the charge today would have been a bit different.

DOC EVATT

Herbert de Vere Evatt was a most distinguished Doctor of Laws who occupied a number of influential positions in the Labor Party in the post-War years. For example, as Minister for External Affairs, he was responsible for Australia's policy towards the United Nations, and in fact was President of the General Assembly when it passed its epoch-making rules on Human Rights. From 1951, he was leader of the Labor Party, and in that role, he was always playing second fiddle to the Leader of the Coalition forces, Prime Minister, Bob Menzies.

At this time, in 1960, he became prominent because it was well known that the position of Chief Justice of the NSW Supreme Court was available, and it was mooted that he could well be the person chosen to fill the vacancy. This was all very exciting for the Australian electorate. Both

Evatt and Menzies had been in their position for about ten years, and their early enthusiasm to change the world had given way, as it always does, to the drudgery of fixing the mistakes they had just made. So the idea of a political shake-up was most welcome.

However, not everyone was happy with Evatt going to the Supreme Court. Letters poured to the Press, and the matter became very lively. The earlier Letters generally were from Labor stalwarts, who were intent on convincing the world that Evatt was a great man, that his record was unimpeachable, and that he was the right man for any job. The later published Letters were somewhat more critical.

Letters, Bruce Maidman. Dr Evatt had a most distinguished career for a large part of his life, and in view of your earlier Letters, I won't go into this. But in the political sphere, his judgement time and time again has been bad. For example, who can forget how he leapt to the defence of the Communists in the Petrov Royal Commission. Here he was the leader of the Labor Party that was suspect for its loyalty to Australian Communists, yet he rushed in and defended them. Whether they had a good cause is not important. The Labor Party was being hounded by Menzies for its close association with the Communists, and still Evatt went to fight its battles.

So, I say his judgement is bad. On top of that, he is completely political. He is a Labor man through and through. Can anyone guarantee that he will be fair and impartial as a judge in his decisions if Labor interests are involved? **Will he perhaps get**

off the Bench and take the position of Advocate for those Labor interests?

It is too risky. There are plenty of other sensible sober judges with a good record who can be appointed. Why risk it with a temperamental, partisan ex-politician with dubious ability to make sound judgements?

Letters, Justin Rickard. It is a sad commentary on the political and moral conscience of this community that the question of the appointment of a Chief Justice can be treated in such a cavalier and opportunist fashion with hardly a voice being raised in horrified protest.

We are not concerned here with Head of the Watermelon Board, or a brand new Chief of the Paspalum Commission, for which offices a disused politician or party faithful would no doubt be admirably qualified, but rather are we dealing with the most senior judicial position in the State, the ultimate protection of the legal rights and privileges of each individual citizen or corporation.

No one in the Labor Party has seriously attempted to deny the fact that the motive behind the move to appoint Dr Evatt to the post arises from the conviction in the minds of his own party that he is of no more use to it. They all attempt to justify his appointment by drawing attention to his undoubted academic qualifications and to his professional achievements.

But you cannot escape the fact that the Labor desire to rid itself of a somehow embarrassing colleague should be placed before the right of the people of NSW to a judiciary of assured impartiality.

With characteristic ineptness, the State Liberal Opposition has lamentably failed to realise the importance of the principle at stake, and has been unwilling to force the Government to a show-down on this issue. Once again, it has failed those whose support it so desperately seeks and needs.

Perhaps the fault is in ourselves, and both the Government and the Opposition alike are but the reflections of a people's attitude of moral compromise and political apathy. Protest we might over a sixpenny increase in the Bridge toll, but the Chief Justice – who's he.

Letters, Norman Oakesy. The legal profession, of which I am a member, is justly proud of the record of independent and impartial members of the Judiciary in all jurisdictions.

The Government does not attempt to intervene in the appointment by the Churches of their own head, nor of the medical profession. It has no more right to arrogate to itself the appointment of a Chief Justice. It should be for the legal profession only, who have to appear in the courts, and in particular the Bar Council, which is more eminently qualified than any other body, to decide upon the most appropriate person to occupy such a high position.

TIME FOR A JAM SESSION

I know I said that I would not keep talking about the Cold War, but bear with me just this once while I point out to you one small by-play that you might not have thought of.

News item, London. The BBC has announced that its daily radio broadcasts to Russia have **not** been jammed by the Russians over the last few days. The broadcasts are in the English language and, for example, last night included a talk from Prime Minister McMillan on racial policy in Capetown, and another on the position of old people in Britain.

The relaxation is a result of the new Anglo-Soviet Cultural Relations Pact recently signed by both countries. Last year, the Russians reduced jamming for the US during Mr Khruschev's visit to that country.

Comment. Needless to say, all this broadcasting and jamming went both ways, and the broadcasts were mainly propaganda in nature.

FRUIT BARROWS IN THE CITY

Letters, Tommy Baker, Balmain. There is greatly increased pressure on the selling of our fruit and vegetables overseas, and we are certain to lose some of these markets. Thus it is all the more important that we sell produce at home. Fruit barrows in the cities do just that. If there are some factors that some people object to, then we should look at them and try to fix up the ones that need fixing. But we should leave alone anything that is good.

If some people do not like horses, we can use some trucks. If some people say the horses are badly treated, they should first of all prove that, and then, if they ever do, we can catch the guilty. If they say we block traffic, ask people if they want better traffic flow or do they want cheap and really fresh fruit and vegetables. What ever the problem, we should fix it. But just do not say that we should get rid of the barrows because big commercial interests have wound us up to say so.

Give the little man a go.

Letters, Jim Scott, NSW Retail Fruit and Vegetable Assn, Sydney. Mr Baker's Letter is supported by a mass of inaccuracies. He knows that the City Council removed 24 barrows from the City a few years ago. Obstruction of traffic was given as a reason. Those in the industry know that malpractice and public health probably played a part in the mass removal.

He talks about the helping out with Australia's over- seas markets. The amount that barrows sell is so small it does not matter, and can have not one iota of effect on overseas markets.

The fact is that 99 per cent of growers' top-quality produce is sold to retailers, providores, country buyers and agents. Half of one per cent is sold to barrows, and this is left-over rubbish. It should not be sold to the public at all. Buying it in 50 or 60 case lots cheaply, some dealers look upon the barrow business as pocket money, tax free, no receipts and no questions asked.

Mr Baker apparently wants a return to the antediluvian age of distribution when nobody cared so long as they made a big profit and the housewife was the last goat in the line.

SYDNEY - MELBOURNE RIVALRY

Letters, E Gill, North Sydney. Here is one Sydneyan who is not altogether depressed to hear that the Victorian police have ordered the removal of Melbourne's "Paris-style" footpath cafes. Personally, I much prefer Collins Street looking like Collins Street, and not a feeble imitation of the Rue Royale.

When are we going to stop this infantile aping of foreign styles and try for a change to initiate some of our own? Mass communication and cheap travel are gradually levelling all the big and little differences between towns and countries.

FRANCE JOINS THE ATOM-BOMB CLUB

The major powers in the world formed a cosy little club that had one thing in common. They each had a supply of working atom bombs of one sort or another.

Each of these was keen to ensure that other nations did not get such devices, so the Big Three, UK, USA and Russia kept their bomb secrets close to their chests.

But France now had somehow advanced its knowledge so that it too was allowed to join the club.

But alas for Bob Menzies, Australia was not. And it never was either.

MARCH: NOT AT ALL POST HASTE

In 1960, the Post Master General, Mr Davidson, an elected Cabinet Minister, and an Officer of the Federal Government, had responsibility for all the mail services in the nation, **and for telephone services**. It was an extensive portfolio that, at this time, was being made more difficult by the rapid changes that were occurring to telephone technology.

For example, women telephone operators across the nation were being sacked, and replaced by automated new systems that, for the first time, used an all-digit number for dialling. Also, various new cables were being laid that would automate trunk calls between the capital cities, and allow the transmission of television signals at the same time.

The general public, however, had little sympathy for the PMG and his Department. Over the last year, his Postal Services had **cut mail deliveries from twice a day to once,** and it **had closed Post Offices on Saturdays.** At the same time, it had raised the price of stamps and just about everything. By March, the heavy criticism that came after the price rises had stopped, and things were settling down to a steady grizzle, when on the 19th , two Letters to the Sydney Morning Herald, criticising the **quality** of the services provided, opened a huge can of worms.

Letters, W Dullo. I feel compelled to say that the rise in postal fees has been accompanied by an appalling deterioration in the standard of services.

Within the last few moths there were lost in my mail within the metropolitan area: a doctor's bill, a set of elaborate working drawings, which had to be repeated at great expense of time, and a letter to Canberra. The doctor whose bill was lost also has observed a deterioration in service, and the addressees of the work drawings say the same, adding that they recently found in the gutter near their business address several letters addressed to them containing cheques.

These facts make further comment unnecessary, but if all those who have had similar experiences come forward, they might force into activity those men who seem to think their duty is done when, from time to time, they reach into their shelves to send out a few more of those ready-prepared letters saying the "the inconvenience caused is regretted."

As to telephone services, the number of failures to connect upon dialling and of wrong connections on inward and outward calls, already numerous before, recently have increased considerably.

If the surplus earned by the Postmaster-General's department was used radically to improve services, I for one would not complain of the PMG's increased charges.

Letters, Phoney Calls. To keep a check on telephone calls I paid 1/- a month (now 1/6) to have a daily record kept at the GPO, and a list forwarded to me monthly. I keep a strict account in my home. For the first half-year of their recording, I was charged for 200 calls which were not made. Since then the number has grown out of all reason.

I am a widow alone in the house most days while my family are at their work, and many evenings while they are at lectures; I have no business or other interests which would necessitate my using the telephone for other than personal reasons. Yet the number of calls recorded against my number included in my last account, 11, 14, 16, 19, 21, 24, 28, 29 and 32 calls on different days. These figures are repeated regularly.

I have written, I have had phone conversations about the matter, and have always been told the meter is in order.

The account, which has risen from 13 Pounds to 33 Pounds for the half-year, is absolutely crippling. If the meter is in order, how can there be such a discrepancy between the meter reading and one's tally?

These Letters unleashed a vast store of resentment among readers, not only of the Herald, but of others from all across the nation. The tirade of abuse was extensive enough to take up half the Letters Page for the rest of the month, and the last Letter received on the subject came through on April 5th.

Letters, DISSATISFIED. Last Easter we were away for four days, and the house was locked up, yet there were six calls registered in those days. When we complained, an inspector called and asked if a maid was employed. As there was no maid, I was then informed that someone must have broken in and used the phone. But, as everything was intact, this was an impossibility.

Phone Bills only come every six months. Why can't they come more often, so that we have a chance of remembering things that happen? Well, I know why.

Letters, R Adams. In the past few months, a gift parcel between two Post Offices only four miles apart was lost by the Department. Another from Adelaide to our P.O was, for some unaccountable reason, "returned to sender." Then it bounced back from Adelaide, and took three weeks all up to deliver. Then transfer forms for shares were delayed for 10 days in the mail, but the distance was only seven miles. Finally, a letter from Melbourne containing a cheque was delivered to the wrong address. Every article was clearly and correctly addressed.

I believe that the duties assigned to junior postal workers are often beyond their educational level, experience, and sense of responsibility. Postmasters and senior officers have to take the impact of resultant complaints by the public, and it is against the interests of the young employees themselves to have excessive responsibility thrust upon them.

Letters, L Irvine. I returned two weeks ago from a visit to India, during which my mail was re-directed by the routine service to my address in New Delhi. The terminal date of the re-direction service was clearly stated on the application form.

A few days ago I made the exasperating discovery that all my mail, which included business and private letters, money and photographic films, was still being sent to India, although the termination date was more than a month ago. There is no remedy in the system for this, and no compensation.

F Cashman, Balmain. My wife sent by registered mail a parcel to a town near Sydney. A week went by, and the parcel had not been delivered. Upon complaint, the Post Master informed my wife that she had to pay a ninepenny search fee to find out what had happened to it.

Would you not agree that the PMG makes a big enough profit without charging the public for its own lack of service?

Letters, Oft Stranded. The postal authorities apparently do not regard service to the public and business as a vitally important matter. I was shocked recently to find that at North Sydney Post Office, no clearances were made between 6 pm and 10.30 am.

By this time, the PMG Department was moving into full denial mode. Dozens of spokesmen round the nation were saying that the service was virtually infallible, and that if a mistake was pointed out, that it was investigated and rectified immediately. But the Letter writers were not at all convinced. The Letters kept pouring in.

Letters, K.D.D. Some time ago, my car registration expired. A week prior to the date I posted in the papers and cheque and promptly forgot the matter. Four weeks later I was booked for driving an unregistered car, and displaying an expired label.

Upon application at the Transport Department, I was informed that there was no record of receipt of such a cheque. I then had to have the car re-inspected, and paid a fresh cheque, obtaining a label on the spot. Later that day, I stopped payment of the first cheque.

About 10 days later I received by post a second label. About four days later this was followed by an abrupt letter advising that it was a serious offence to register the same car twice, and demanding return of the label within 24 hours, followed by threats of certain penalties. Upon later application to obtain the "stopped" cheque, I was advised that it could not be given to me "as it was required for consideration of further legal action against me" – for what?

Letters, NOT SURPRISED On Eight-hour Day, last October, I sent colour films from Bathurst to Melbourne, and not receiving them back by the end of November, I wrote to the PMG Department about them. I was told they had made enquiries and could not locate the missing films. Much to my surprise, I received them, correctly addressed, in the middle of February, and postmarked in Abbotsford, Victoria on October 13, 1959. Thus over four months elapsed before delivery. We seem to pay more for less these days.

By now the Post Master General himself was under daily attack in Parliament, and all he could do was to squirm and say that occasionally human mistakes had been made in the past, but from now on, supervision would be tightened even more. At the same time, the Department decided it was time to make refunds. An interesting feature of these sudden bursts of generosity was that, as the days wore on they became less precise. That is, initially the deduction was down to the last penny. Then it was measured to the last Shilling, a few days later it got down to the Pound. Finally, it came in round numbers. "Your bill has been reduced by 10 Pounds."

KDD of Elizabeth Bay had a billing of 67 Pounds reduced to 17 Pounds, a mere 50 Pounds difference. **Mrs J Peterson, from Ashbury** wrote that she had received her account earlier in March. "I was astounded that I had been charged 87 Pounds and eightpence. I complained, and the locals sent me an amended account for 3 Pounds and 14 Shillings. This overcharge of 83 Pounds was the biggest I have heard of so far."

Comment.   Yes, Mrs Peterson, I agree that it is quite impressive. But in percentage terms, you are up against **Mr Grunsted from Wyong,** who was informed that "the bill that was originally stated to be forty-one Pounds, four Shillings and two Pence, had on appeal been reduced to three Shillings and ten Pence."

This type of abuse went on and on. Every day for three weeks an average of 24 column-inches were printed by the Herald. On two days, the Letters spilled out on to separate quarter-page spreads of concentrated frustration and contempt. One forward-thinking writer said the solution was to invite corporations from overseas to come in and offer competition for the PMG. But this type of thinking was well ahead of anything we were prepared to consider.

So, after a while, the Services went back to normal, and there was no shake up really until they were split, into Australia Post on one hand, and Telstra on the other late in the Century.

Comment. I would not want to do the PMG's job. Not then in 1960, nor now that it has been split in two. Hundred of thousands of employees, with the inevitable misfits. Billions of letters and phone calls, every one of vital importance to the originator. Add to that the rapid changes in technology, and the constant fighting with Government.

But having said that, there was no doubt that the Department did have a number of self-satisfied employees who felt that they could perform indifferently and still keep their jobs. They were bolstered in this attitude by the lack of any form of competition. It was the perfect monopoly, and it acted pretty much as monopolies were supposed to.

BIG TROUBLE IN SOUTH AFRICA

On March 23, the Press here reported that rioting had been widespread in South Africa the previous day. The ostensible cause was that the black population were now being forced to carry identity passes that were deemed to interfere with their human rights and natural freedoms. The white population was largely spared from this requirement.

On this day, the events and their reportage was confused. It is clear that at about a dozen mainly urban centres, blacks who opposed the passes had organised to meet and publicly protest against them. At many of these places, the meetings got out of hand, and the mixture of excited and angry blacks on the one hand, and frightened and aggressive police and white citizens on the other, resulted in extremes of violence.

The most serious of these was at **Sharpville,** a township 30 miles outside Johannesburg. There, 58 people were shot and killed when a mob besieged and stoned a police station. One hundred and sixty other people were seriously wounded. At another location, Langra, 6,000 Africans gathered in the square in front of the police station to sing the National Anthem. Fighting broke out as armoured cars and police vans arrived with reinforcements. Sten guns were used to turn them away, some of the Africans fired back, and riots developed all over the town from there. Seven buildings were set ablaze, including the Town Hall and two schools. Dozens of other blacks were killed across the nation. One white man was said to be dead.

The blacks had no doubt about the cause. One was reported as saying "the police came here today to kill us. That is what they did." Another report, which may or not be true, said the local police Commander at Sharpville, Colonal J Piernaar, pointed to the three-inch scratch on his car, and said "my car was struck by a stone. If they want to do these things, they must learn their lesson the hard way."

Commentary on the **now-famous Sharpville Massacre** was quite unfavourable to the white police. The London Times referred to the pass system as "the visible signs of a highly complicated and frankly tyrannical network of control." The London Daily Mirror said that "yesterday's tragedy could be the beginning of revolt in South Africa". A correspondent to the Times said that "it could be the end of the British Empire."

Violence continued in small pockets for about two weeks then it flared up again on March 30 in Capetown itself. Overnight, more than 50 white, black and coloured leaders of the fight against segregation were arrested in raids on their homes. A protest of 30,000 people filled the streets with men and women protesting, and then rioting and shooting followed. A State of Emergency was declared in troubled areas, and the Prime Minister, Mr Verwoerd, warned Africans that if their demonstrations became more violent, they would be met with greater force. On the same day, nine Sydney students were arrested during a 1,000-student demonstration in the city against the developing campaign of apartheid in South Africa.

The Sydney Morning Herald that day published a Letter that presented clearly the case of the Africans in strong and moving terms.

Letters, Richard Arvidson, Johannesburg, South Africa. I am a young man, 22 years of age. My youth has been spent largely in South Africa, where I witnessed the cruel network of racial legislation in action, which has thrown my country into such turmoil.

The recent riots at Sharpeville represent another link in a chain of events, each one more powerful than the last; a chain that threatens to cripple the last vestiges of peace and goodwill that exist between the black and white peoples of this country.

The black peoples are gradually being deprived of their inalienable rights as free human beings and of the last vestiges of human respectability. Here lies the awful danger of South Africa. When men reach such a state, where they have few rights, it can take but a small incident to incite them to violence.

Millions of indigenous Bantu people live barely above the breadline. All facets of this monstrous evil militate against their advancement. We see the degeneration of Christian morality and the democratic way of life that characterises the free civilised community.

Justice has degenerated into a mockery when whites receive small terms of imprisonment, with the option of ridiculously small fines, for such crimes as rape and culpable homicide committed with aggravating circumstances against Bantu, and Bantu receive severe terms of imprisonment for such crimes as petty theft, and banishment without trial on the vaguest suspicions of their political advancement.

All peoples who oppose present Government policy have their freedom of expression restricted. We have restrictions of academic freedom and restrictions of freedom of religion. There is great conflict between the British heritage of English-speaking people and the extreme Afrikaner nationalism. This extremity has led to a system of government which approaches dictatorship.

I have experienced the generation of almost unbelievable tension between the two great colour groups, as well as the fear this tension has inspired.

We are in a state of momentous flux and already witness the beginnings of crumbling of the tyranny of apartheid, with the progressive enlightenment of the white electorate to its intrinsic evils, at a time when men are increasingly concerned with their future as citizens of South Africa in a multi-racial society.

In the dark agony of South Africa we can see the first glimmering of the dawn, and take strength in the belief that Right will ultimately prevail.

LABOUR'S NEW LEADER - AT LAST

After waiting a long time for Doc Evatt to retire from the leadership of the Federal Labor Party, Arthur Calwell was elected to fill his shoes. His appearance remained the same, as if he was choking in stale tobacco. The new Deputy Leader, Gough Whitlam, on the other hand, looked bright eyed and bushy tailed. He was about to start on a ten-year role as understudy, though it was not always clear that he was walking hand in hand with his master.

PREPARATIONS FOR THE ROYAL WEDDING

These were going ahead. The young couple, Princess Margaret and Anthony Armstrong-Jones, will have two possible residences available to them. Kensington Palace could offer them an apartment made up of 30 - 40 rooms. Princess Alexandra already has an apartment in the Palace, and it might be nice to have a relative close and handy when it comes time for baby sitting.

This second residence is favoured as a "Grace and Favour" country house. It's name is Frogmore House, a former

Royal residence in the Home Park of Windsor Castle. It is a Georgian residence with extensive gardens, and will be great for those barbies on Sunday afternoons.

CARS RUN ON SUNSHINE

The world's first solar car was on display in New York. It needs eight hours of sunlight to propel it for one hour. It has a panel of silicon voltaic cells on its roof. These cells at the moment cost 9,600 dollars, but the price could come down to 900 dollars.

BIG MONTH FOR THE POLICE

The NSW Police were moving with the times. Firstly, the Commissioner, Mr Delaney, was considering fitting police cars in the State with **sirens.** The argument for them was that they had been found effective in Victoria in getting cars through heavy traffic. However, a Parliamentary Representative for Liverpool, Mr Wrightley, said that they would frighten drivers of other vehicles, adding to the confusion, and slow down the police. Mr Delaney was also considering **the introduction of seat belts** in Police cars.

Mr Delaney also announced, under new regulations, women can remain in the police force **after** they get married. Women will now enter the Force on the same conditions as men, and can reach the rank of sergeant.

A NEW POM NOT QUITE HAPPY

Letters, Fred Prior, Palm Beach. I have only a month ago arrived at your wonderful country from England.

I was baffled on Saturday. I went with my wife and another lady and attended a public luncheon at one of your higher-class hotels. I invited the two ladies to have an aperitif, and escorted them to the hotel lounge. When I ordered the sherries, I was told by the waiter that "sherry was not served in the lounge". I have since found out that sherry, port and brown muscat are considered drinks fit for only drunks, and are all sold for consumption in brown paper bags.

This is a real shock to me because the image presented in London is that Australian sherry is consumed only by the most sophisticated people.

It is very disappointing.

WERE THE YANKS GOODIES OR BADDIES?

American influence was everywhere in this nation. In the movies, in our music, in our clothing, our slang, our politics, our cars, our miitary, our TV, our News services, our food, and all things great and small.

One question that came out of this was whether we were destined to become another State of the great USA. After all, it was argued by some, we were drifting away from Britain quickly, but we still needed a strong supporter. There was only the USA who could fulfill this role.

What about it? Just roll with the punches.

APRIL: APRIL FOOLS' DAY?

On April 1st, Australians were treated to a preview of Time Magazine's portrait of Prime Minister, Robert Gordon Menzies. This particular day was very popular in those years for the playing of practical jokes on all and sundry. When the portrait appeared on this morning, many people thought that here again they were being the victims of some giant set-up.

It wasn't the painter. **He** was not under suspicion. He was the renowned William Dobell. Nor was it was the great and lofty Bob Menzies. Rather, it was the whole concept of art itself. Surely, many argued, a painting of a person should look like the person. It should not look like some caricature, or some cartoon sketch. Really, it must look just like the man himself, warts and all, precisely. Equally, others said that portraits should present faithful images of the sitter. Otherwise, just fantasise.

So, April got off to a good start. Here was a topic where everyone had an opinion, and everyone could suddenly become an expert on the theory of art.

Letters, Weaver Hawkins. People do not seem to see the obvious: that the strongest influence on William Dobell, our great portrait painter, is and always has been Rembrandt, that genius of the long past before man had been enabled to allow **his human vision to be perverted by the camera.**

Mr Dobell has to an extraordinary degree been able as an artist to retain that power of depicting forcefully his true impression of the sitter in addition to making a fine picture of a portrait.

Letters, Caroline Gillespie, Cammeray. Dobell's portrait is shocking. It looks much more like Alfred Hitchcock than Menzies, and a critically ill Mr Hitchcock at that!

Letters, J Ayling. My dictionary, an old one admittedly, defines a portrait as a "likeness in oil or watercolours" and surely the only reason for spending large sums of money on portraits of prominent people is to present them as they actually appear. What possible purpose, then, is there in labelling Mr Dobell's arrangements of colour (however interesting they may be) as well-known names?

While one may sympathise with Mr Dobell if he really sees human beings as he depicts them, it seems most unfair to deceive a future age in this way, for on present indications they will be confused and bewildered enough as things are.

Letters, George Grahame. People see portraits differently. Some say an artist should paint the subject exactly as he looks, and others say he should muck about as much as he likes. They should leave each other alone, and accept the fact that people are different. And painters should be free to paint as they like. And judges in painting competitions should also be free to pick what they like. Who are these people who tell others all the time what they should be doing?

This is a free country, and if I'm not trampling on your rhubarb, then leave me alone.

NSW HOSPITALS.

The *Sydney Morning Herald* ran a series of five articles on the faults in the Public Hospitals in NSW. The newspaper was conscious of the number of complaints from Letter-writers about the system, and it set out to test their validity. Its conclusion was that the patient is little more than "an unavoidable nuisance to the modern hospital, that his anxious relatives, restlessly pacing a drab waiting-room or pleading over the phone for news, can easily be brushed off, as indeed they often are." In brief, that consideration for the patient and his kin was sadly lacking.

The articles went on to ask whether the fault lay with doctors, who put private patients ahead of hospital work. Or perhaps with nurses who have abandoned dedication to embrace industrialisation. They argued that hospitals were muddling through with a system that Europe and America would call decadent, and that nurses, doctors and administrators had "pushed a tombstone over Florence Nightingale".

They also asked many leading questions. Is the constant cry for more hospital beds justified, or does Australia already possess too many beds. Are beds used wastefully, and could they be reduced by starting home-nursing services? Does the National Health Service add anything, or does it merely ensure that doctors and hospitals get paid? Do the hospitals use their nurses wisely, or does the system tend to convert trainee-nurses into automata?

Responses to these claims were many and vigorous. Some of these Letters, sometimes edited and truncated, are shown below.

Letters, Aileen Williamson. As it now stands, in many cases these institutions are symbols of clinical hygiene certainly, but also of cold and harsh military discipline. It seems to be an accepted concept that a creaseless counterpane and a bed of impeccable appearance are of more importance to the matron on her rounds than the comfort and condition of the sick person in it. Furthermore, many doctors act as though they were skilled technicians working on a faulty machine.

Letters, G Carr. I know of no sphere of modern life, other than that of hospital nursing, which continues on the level of old-fashioned snobbery and tyranny. If it was not so distressing, it would be laughable. Every little would-be "Caesar", as she rises a step above the others, fits into the set pattern which treats the lower nurse with contempt and humiliating severity. Hospital nursing is a little world of antiquated despotism set apart from the rest of modern life, and no one has told those responsible how much out of touch they are with the twentieth-century.

How can nurses be expected to maintain a balanced and courteous calm at all times under high pressure of work, when they are constantly frustrated and humiliated by bullying and contempt which would not be tolerated in any other walk of life?

Letters, Jean Sheppard. Matrons, and assistant matrons, should make a tour of the wards every day; not with a view to smooth **coverlets** and inspect polished floors, but with the eye of experience on the patients' comfort and with time for a word here or there with a fellow human being. The standard of nursing and approach to the patient is determined by them and cannot be over stressed.

There were many such Letters from people who saw matrons as lacking. Their criticism extended down to senior nurses, who were often called "cold and indifferent" and bullies.

There were also Letters which complained about facilities in the wards and lack of responses in a timely manner. I enclose just one such Letter, though I could fill many pages.

Letters, K Mears. On arrival with a suitcase I was told to report to the hepatitis ward, a quarter of a mile away. I collapsed half-way. An off-duty nurse saw me and helped me the rest of the way. This for an illness that required absolute rest.

The radio was connected to a loud speaker in the ward ceiling and, as young trainee nurses controlled the master set, we got rock 'n' roll from 6 a.m. till 9 p.m. The only time it was turned off was during the doctors' rounds. To ask for it to be turned off was to incur the unofficial but most effective retaliation of the nursing staff.

Hepatitis patients are not allowed out of bed, thus bedpans are necessary. If used at an unusual time they were left un-emptied on the end of the bed for up to an hour. Once again, complaint brought effective unofficial retaliation.

Comments, however, were not all bad. Quite a lot of writers spoke up for some parts of the system. It was obvious that the nurses and doctors who had contact with patients were well regarded, especially if they were able to exercise their humanity freely. The two letters below offer good support.

Letters, SISTER. I am sorry to see Mr Carr's views on Caesars of the wards. He apparently accepts the fallacy that so-called Caesars are bad.

Any nurse worthy of the name knows different. I am the product of a well-known Sydney Caesar-type factory, and in common with fellow trainees look back with deepest gratitude to the strict training given to young girls who were immature and without the necessary sense of responsibility that came with training.

It is a well-known fact of psychology that young people lack a sense of security unless discipline is firm, and nowhere more than in the young student nurse, facing situations that place a heavy strain on most people of maturer years.

Because the nurse is a disciplined person it does not mean she is hounded into the ground, though I know some individuals can misuse their authority. The nurse must be disciplined in life and habit of work in order to do her work satisfactorily. May I add that it is one of the best character-forming occupations there is if the student nurse, backed by religious faith and training to steady her, is prepared to be moulded by it.

May I point out that underneath those Caesar exteriors beat hearts of understanding, with a desire to help young girls passing through the experience they once did, and to produce the type of nurse we all so badly need.

Letters, R Williams. Your anonymous correspondent deserves more than the praise lavished on him for his articles on the abuses in the medical system. Might I suggest that, as a reward, he be given the opportunity of writing an on-the-spot feature?

Surely it can be arranged for him to experience some of the life and work of a nurse, first hand. He could rise at dawn, perhaps clean up a patient incontinent of faeces, or lay out a corpse. How our nurses would benefit from feeling the warmth with which he would help them hold down a violent maniac, or the glint of Nightingale fervour with which he would dress a gangrenous ulcer, perhaps swarming with maggots. Perhaps he could then spend a while with one of the "very young gentlemen with stethoscopes round their necks." Let him stay with him for the full 70 to 90 hours per week, and fall into bed with the knowledge that there is a telephone beside his ear that may or not ring, and then rise to stand, from 8am to 8pm, heavily gowned, under the hot theatre arc lamps.

Let him feel more of the patients he is championing, as they lurch off their bunks to lie in a pool of their urine, shouting obscenities at those who try to help them. And one prerequisite must be mentioned. For this period you must pay him the same wage as the trainee nurse and the resident doctor receive.

The articles simply make the need for better facilities an excuse for an unjustified, patronising insult to the most overworked, underpaid and yet invaluable section of the community.

SMH **Editor's comment.** This letter calls for comment since it admirably illustrates a widespread attitude discovered by our staff correspondent.in his investigation. That is, what is wrong with the hospital is the patients. Dr Williams says that much nursing work is dirty and unpleasant and that many doctors work very hard. This is well known, nor did the articles deny it. But an attitude that implies, as it does, that the typical patients are mad, drunk, obscene, incontinent or gangrenous goes far to explain the lack of sympathy of which so many hospital patients complain.

SOUTH AFRICA: YEARS OF CONFLICT

The month started with violence and ended with violence. On the first day, police fired on marching Africans in two cities, Durban and Johannesburg, killing three. They also made baton charges into a mob rioting in a beer hall at Natalspruit, killed one African who was with a gang stoning trains, and arrived too late to protect a church that was burnt down at Uitenhage, and a dozen other schools, and a radio station, right across the country.

This pattern of unpredictable, sporadic series of provocations and retaliations was to continue for months and months and months. At the moment, there was nothing organised about it. Just people fed up with being the not-haves, now being goaded by new laws that threatened to make permanent and official the policies of separation, and for them, exclusion. All of this was overlaid on a bleak history of white oppression and African subjugation, in a society where the wealth and power and positions of authority were in the hands of the imported white man.

The rest of the world looked on with various measures of concern. The United Nations Security Council, with a large share of emerging black nations, clearly condemned the South African Government, and called for sanctions. Leaders from Commonwealth countries, who felt they had a special right to speak because of their Commonwealth links, generally also condemned the Government.

Prime Minister, Bob Menzies, was more conservative. He argued that the rioting and violence were part of the internal affairs of a sovereign nation, and that Australia had no right to interfere there. But behind that convenient excuse, he could see that, throughout the world and the British Commonwealth, there were dozens of other nations who were poised to go the same way.

For him to come out and say that the blacks were the innocent victims, and the white man was the cruel oppressor, would have been tantamount to encouraging liberation movements across the world. Not only that, he could scarcely say that our own occupation, and economic exploitation, of New Guinea was above scrutiny. So, he kept his peace, along with President Eisenhower, and said as little controversial as possible. But, whether spoken out loud or not, it was clear that the white man in South Africa was seen as the villain. But the system they had set up was not without its supporters.

Letters, Peter Ferguson. As a South African, I am deeply disturbed by some of the opinions on the recent shooting in Sharpville. We have been told that "thousands of Africans were told to assemble outside a police station, and when they did, the police turned their machine–guns on them." But is this the truth?

The South African Government has said it is not. It says that the police fired only after they were fired on first. It asks whether "it was asking too much of a small group of policemen to commit suicide." If this statement is true, it obviously throws a different light upon the incident.

As the recent riots have arisen out of the pass system, we should ask whether this is a system that enslaves and chains the Africans, as claimed?

Well, far from being a chain, the pass system was designed for the African's own protection. **First**, to many Africans in the countries adjoining South Africa, the Union is a welfare state. They are attracted there by good wages, health provisions, education and so on. There are a million illegal immigrants in the country now.

Second, the cities are attracting hundreds of thousands of people, and this has led to appalling shanty towns. Here, thousands of unemployed Africans maintain a parasitic existence off their fellow man. For this reason, the pass system was brought in, whereby all illegal immigrants were deported, and the unemployed in the cities were sent back to their reserves which occupy the rich and fertile Eastern grassland.

The result of this is that the standard of living of the urban African has been notably raised. For example, Sophiatown has vanished, and beautiful Meadowtown, a modern suburb for Africans, has taken its place. No longer can the unscrupulous employer dictate his terms to the African, as he could when there was a surplus of available labour.

These recent riots have no connection with apartheid, and this is borne out by separate statements of both the Pan-Africanists and the African National Congress.

A very interesting view of things. But just when you thought it was now all sorted out, up pop a few writers who think they know different.

Letters, H Frochwaig. Mr Ferguson talks about the benefits natives derived from the move from Sophiatown to the beautiful modern suburb of Meadowtown. He really must know that many natives actually owned the freehold of these very attractive cottages, which they had paid off by mortgage over many years. By Government decree they were all forced to abandon them, in all cases without compensation, and were forced to take up residence at Meadowtown.

Has Mr Ferguson seen Meadowtown? It is designed and controlled as a concentration camp. The natives may only enter or leave by a police-controlled gate. All residents must be in camp by nightfall. All visitors must first receive a permit. Sanitary conditions within the camp are appalling.

Any gathering by Africans, even weddings, where 10 or more guests assemble, has to have police permission and a police officer has to be present to make notes of conversations. Those expressing anti-Government opinions are liable to arrest.

Letters, Mark Braham. Under the Western Areas Removal Scheme, 60,000 Africans were forcibly evicted from Sophiatown. Some families who had lived there for forty tears were given 10 hours notice to move.

The London *Times* described this as "not only a moral horror but a deliberate attempt to increase African insecurity". Major newspapers around the world echoed this opinion.

Meanwhile, things were not getting better in South Africa. The *Sydney Morning Herald* leader of April 6th told us that:

South African police, armed with whips, clubs and sticks, and supported by armoured cars and troops, are out in force in Capetown again today trying to beat the Africans back to work. The police swept into the African township of Nyagana, near Capetown, early this morning. There, Africans who refused orders to leave the houses were pulled out and beaten up, an African said.

Shots were fired when groups of Africans attempted to resist the police, and at least five Africans were reported to be wounded by gunfire. One non-white constable was hacked to death, and two white policemen were wounded. It was the second day of beatings in an attempt to compel the natives to end their anti-white work boycott. Many had whip-lash injuries on the back and other parts of the body. Most of the wounded had bullets in their legs or thighs.

On the 9th of April, South African Prime Minister, Dr Hendrik Verwoerd, attended an agricultural Show, and after looking at the display, was prepared to speak to a seated audience. He did that, vowing the South Africa "will never hand over control of this nation to a black majority".

Soon after, a lone gunman, posing as a member of the Show committee, stepped onto the podium and **fired two shots into the head of Verwoerd**. He was severely wounded and stretchered away to hospital. The gunman was captured and beaten and sent off with the police. Verwoerd recovered after some anxious moments, and resumed his duties a few weeks later. But his vow of never surrendering remained unchanged, and the violence continued unabated throughout.

Letters, Rev Alex Richards. Writing as an Afrikaner, I have to confess a sense of shame at developments in South Africa. Opinion is divided even among South Africans as to the correctness of apartheid, but I imagine I echo the astonishment of many Afrikaners living abroad when I express amazement at the use of whips in the present circumstances.

Those who are part of South Africa understand the fear in the white mind that the African will one day take his revenge for much of the treatment meted out to him over the past 150-200 years. That retaliation (as every white South African knows is capable of taking a form peculiar to the African thinking – a form not pleasant to contemplate. It is understandable that the South African Government should use force in the present situation, and that its parliamentary Opposition should support that move; but that whips should be used ---!

Buried deep in the African memory is the experience of those same whips used during last century. Almost more than any other indignity the African remembers that. It passes comprehension that a South African Government should endorse the use of whips in the present situation.

These are no ordinary whips. The rhinoceros-hide sjambok of South Africa has few equals in the world for inflicting punishment or for impressing a lesson of inferiority. Whatever the pass system and apartheid may previously have been, they must now in the African mind be associated.

Undoubtedly the South African Government will bring the present situation under control and undoubtedly the question of apartheid (and its attendant problems) is a domestic one at the moment; but anyone who knows even some of the basic facts behind this racial tension can doubt that it must eventually overflow in the international sphere, "when the African lion awakes..."

The African is not a "nigger" or a "kaffir" or a dog. He is a fellow man. He has as much a part in the redemptive work of Christ as has the white man. Archbishop Joost de Blank, of Capetown, has voiced an opinion which challenges the whole Christian world. "...the African cannot be blamed for feeling that Christian love has no meaning."

I submit that it is true to say that love in Christ is the only complete answer to this and every other racial problem, including that of Australian aboriginal integration. But is there sufficient time left to demonstrate the proof of it?

Comment. What a terribly difficult situation. The white, mainly Dutch, population had been in the country for hundreds of year, and their labour and capital had played an enormous role in its development. They did not want the forces of equity and democracy to take away any part of this.

On the other hand, the Africans, in their various groups and tribes, wanted to get their hands on the wealth and power in their own country. It was a situation that was being faced all over the world as native populations were seeking self-determination, and to get rid of the imperial powers that had ruled them for many years. It was similar in the US, where the blacks were fighting for rights. There was no simple solution, and in fact, not even a complicated one.

Each country has since then made some sense of their own problems and things have changed slowly over the last fifty years. In South Africa's case, the fact was that the Government was better organised to exercise more control, so ironically it could be more systematically repressive. And it was just that, it appears. It would have been better for that Government to follow the relatively more enlightened approach of the British, and indeed the Dutch in Indonesia, but once the repression started, it was impossible to stop, and over the years, it bred more violence and long-remembered hatreds that have ruled conduct for decades.

A SECOND OZ PIONEER

Ben Boyd is one of those legendary figures of Australia that everyone has heard of, but can't quite remember why they are famous. This gentleman was an English entrepreneur who came to Australia with a lot of money, bought up lots of land, spent big and lavishly and, after about ten years, sailed away a lot poorer than he arrived. Nothing too special here, but in that process, he established a number of whaling stations, and in the boom years for whaling from 1820 to 1850, he turned Twofold Bay into the centre of that now-dubious industry. That's why we hazily remember him.

Letters, L Wright. The history related to me by the chief of Sugu, the main village in Wanderer Bay in the south-west corner of Guadalcanal, where Boyd was killed, was that the yacht Wanderer anchored in the bay and at first the crew went ashore without molestation. Later, Boyd, with two or three companions, went exploring up the small river near the village, watched with trepidation by the natives since this river led to a hill regarded as sacred.

There was an urgent meeting of the villagers, and it was decided that the risk was too great of the party violating the taboo, with dire results to the people. The warriors were therefore instructed to wipe out the party, and it was speared to death.

The sequel was the landing of the Wanderer's crew, the shooting of some natives and burning of the village, which was interrupted by a sudden squall causing a hurried re-embarkation and the sailing of the yacht to a safer anchorage.

These facts were related to me, when district officer of Guadalcanal, by the old chief who was born less than 20 years after the event when the circumstances were still vivid in the people's minds.

Boyd's death resulted from the same cause responsible for the annihilation of the Australian expedition to Tatuve years later – the fear that the white man was about to desecrate ground sacred to the ancestral spirits whose wrath would be vented on the people.

A SOLUTION TO THE POSTMAN'S WOES

Letters, F Luke, Normanhurst. It gave me great pleasure to find that at last someone has come to the defence of dogs who bite postmen. I think the writer is on the right track in stating that dogs are almost human in intelligence. This being so, it is obvious that dogs must recognise certain postmen as bad eggs and are the only beings with enough gumption to take action. Therefore, instead of destroying the dog, why not destroy the postman?

FLORIDE IN TOOTHPASTE

The American Dental Association has for the first time ever officially recognised a toothpaste as an effective agent against tooth decay. It had been found in extensive testing that brushing with floride toothpaste reduced cavities generally by about 50 per cent, compared to other pastes. The Association went on to say that floride in drinking water was far better than this, but for communities without floride in their drinking water, this paste was a good alternative.

NEW MARBLES FOR LOTTERIES

News Item, August 5, Sydney. The State Lotteries Office of NSW has ordered a new set of wooden marbles to replace a present set that is twenty years old. The Acting Director of State Lotteries said that the set was ordered because of the discovery of a chipped marble in Lottery Number 4579 last Wednesday.

The marble, Number 43667, one of 100,000, came out with the middle digit partly chipped away. The damaged marble had been destroyed and replaced. All remaining marbles were in good health.

MAY: GARY POWERS AND THE SPY-PLANE

Over the last few months, the ON-again OFF-again Cold War had switched to OFF. Everyone had been nice to each other for about a month. Heads of States had made lots of visits and apparently some hope that the long-standing arguments about the fate of Germany would be settled. As one American paper said, "things are all hunky-dory, sweety-pie".

The leaders of the bigger Powers were all packing their bags to go to a Summit Conference in Paris. The newspapers said that hopes were reportedly high that, if only the chiefs of State could get together face-to-face, they might settle on some plans about disarmament and about the future of Berlin. Of course, this was a lot of hot air. Nearly everyone knew that the aims of the two major players, Russia and America, were diametrically opposed and, at dozens of places round the world, they were in no-holds-barred economic and propaganda wars with each other. But the headlines and politicians kept pumping away at it, so it was building to a big occasion.

Well, it **was** too good to last. On Thursday May 5th, the leaders of the Russians were pleased to announce to the Russian Parliament that an American spy-plane had been shot down over Soviet territory. This caused havoc that spread in all directions. **Firstly**, the world asked of America, was it true that such planes existed, and that they were being used to spy on sovereign nations? Were they spying on other countries? Or **all** countries? On our country?

Secondly, the U2 Lockheed would have been flying at close to 65,000 feet. Did the Russians have rockets or planes that could reach that height? After all, the US had long been bragging that they were in sole control of such devices. Was the military superiority of the US just a giant propaganda lie?

Thirdly, and Mr K hammered this point home, did the flights have the permission of the President Eisenhower? If they did, how could Mr K trust him to tell the full truth at meetings? Could the coming Summit achieve anything if the chief capitalist protagonist was preaching ethical conduct, and yet not practising it? Can you trust such a man? And if the flights did not have Ike's permission, who was calling the shots in the US? He speculated that it could be Richard Nixon. Nixon would be the "last person to think of stopping the Cold War because it would mean the end of the Arms Race." He went on to say that if Nixon at some stage stood in for Ike at the Summit, it would be "like sending a goat to take care of a cabbage".

The US State Department gathered itself together and after a day said that the "bandit plane" was an unarmed weather-study craft whose civilian pilot might have blacked out. However, photographs taken from the crashed plane indicated that without a doubt he was spying on Soviet military installations.

The State Department had no choice. The next day they admitted that it was a spy plane. They added that it was not authorised by Washington, and that enquiries were continuing to determine just who did give it approval. It also admitted to two such flights each week for the last four years! The American public were horrified by these admissions. The Washington Correspondent of the New York Times sums it up when he wrote "Washington is a sad and perplexed capital tonight, caught in a swirl of charges of clumsy administration, bad judgement, and bad faith. The Government is embarrassed by being caught red-handed spying 1,600 miles into the Soviet, and trying to cover up its activities in a series of misleading official statements."

But, even in the face of such adversity, the US had at least one friend.

Letters, M Towner. Is there none who will join with me in happy congratulations to the Americans that for once in this long Cold War we are showing that the Russians are not always permitted to fight on the battleground of their own choosing?

The forward patrols are out once more, and if we are to be attacked tonight, tomorrow or next week, we can be sure of some warning.

While nervous neutrals and fearful friends may tremble in fear of offending the bully, there will be many in the world who will be grateful that America has demonstrated her intention of containing the Communist imperialists.

The men who direct and fly these missions in unarmed aircraft to ensure that there will be no second Pearl Harbour show bravery of the highest order, and should be assured of the highest appreciation and gratitude of the Australian public and free men everywhere.

Not a great atmosphere for starting a Summit. But, as it turned out, no one had to worry about what happened at the Summit, because, at the first opportunity, at 8 a.m. on the first day, Mr Khrushchev announced that he would leave if the Americans did not apologise for the spy-plane incident. They would not do so.

So the Russians packed up and went home, and everyone else decided there was no point in going on without them. The Summit was abandoned and the planned 10-day Paris conference to save the world from nuclear oblivion did not go ahead. Of course, everyone blamed everyone else, but the Australian Letter-writers still had the last say.

Letters, F McElhone. It is now fairly obvious that Mr Khrushchev has never genuinely wanted a summit conference, or for it to succeed.

He has protested too much over the ill-advised USA spy flight over Russia, when that country itself has the most highly organised spy system in the world. Even the spy-plane episode itself takes a lot of explaining away, and there is a strong suspicion that the whole thing was stage-managed in some way.

Mr Khrushchev's uncompromising attitude and outbursts at the summit conference may have been part of a deliberate policy to try to get the Western Allies to make concessions in order to quieten him down. Or he may have received uncompromising directions from the Presidium of the Supreme Soviet itself. Or, what is also likely, Russia's ally, China, which wants the cold war to continue, and does not believe in co-existence, may have given

Russia the strongest possible hints not to agree to any reasonable compromise.

There is, of course, another explanation. Russia speaks with its tongue in its cheek when it talks of co-existence, which is contrary (although a useful tactic) to the basic tenets of Communism, the basic strategy of which is the overthrow of the democratic Governments and the setting up of world communism. This basic strategy should never be forgotten; tactics may vary, but not the fundamental strategy.

Everything therefore points to Russia's having deliberately sabotaged the summit conference in order to continue the Cold War and world tension for its own purposes. At the same time we should not be unduly worried, because a lot of the Russian bluster is merely propaganda. At the same time the democracies must keep united and their defences strong.

Letters, A Dalton. Is it not time that we examined the tragic failure of the Summit collapse from the mentality of the Russian people. In a world in which their country was devastated, where eight million of their people were wiped out, where great works and enterprises, homes, farms were wiped out, there is bound to exist, at all levels, an awful fear of another war.

Consequently, when the stupid and provocative act of the USA in sending a spy plane over Russian territory, from military bases that encircle Russia, is done on the very eve when America is preparing to talk peace, is it any wonder that Russia reacts in a violent manner.

After all, the US has never known modern warfare on its own soil. Surely there is enough sanity in the high places of American government to prevent such acts of calamitous stupidity. Or are there powerful influences at work in America who have too much to lose by a diminution of the Cold War and who wish to see it perpetuated and intensified?

Comment. I think it that there was no need to shed any tears over the failure of the Summit. The differences between the two sides were so great that if it had not been the Powers incident that broke up the Summit, it would have been something else, real or contrived.

Looking ahead a few months, the pilot Powers was subsequently tried by the Russians, for espionage. Here, the penalty if guilty was 15 years imprisonment or death. I will leave you, for the moment, to guess what he got. But we will be back later.

TWO MURDERS IN MAITLAND

On Sunday, April 24, the normal peace and comfort of Sunday mornings was shattered by the news that police had been called to a residence in the country town of East Maitland on the Saturday morning. There they found the lifeless bodies of a young couple, the man in the hallway, and the woman in the bedroom. What distinguished these murders from others was that **in both cases, the head was missing**.

A brother-in-law tells of discovering their bodies, at 9.30 a.m. "We usually take a bottle up to Sid (the male victim) on Saturday. When we got there today, I yelled out, but nobody answered me. The dogs barked and I went to rattle on the door. Then I saw blood on the doorstep. I got a 44-gallon drum and climbed up to the window. Sid was lying in the hallway. His head was missing. I nearly fell into the drum with shock, and was too sick to go inside."

The police arrived, and when they entered they found the second body. The mother of the dead man, Mrs Gladys Shelley, who had been called to open up the house for the police, an hour later found the couple's young daughter in a crib, covered by a pile of blankets and a suitcase. The child was found to be suffering from concussion as a result of a blow to the ear, and was taken to Maitland Hospital.

It was believed at the time that the killer had first shot Mr Shelley, and then beheaded him on the doorstep of their bush home. He then killed Mrs Elva Shelley in the bedroom. A butcher's cleaver was thought to have been used. It was believed that the killer, probably a "psychopath" had left the scene, with the heads, in a car.

Intensive police searches of nearby areas were conducted, and investigations continued throughout the week. But next Sunday, May Day, May the 1st, the newspapers brought another shocking headline. The head of Mrs Elva Shelley had been found floating in Newcastle Harbour, at a wharf at Carrington. A small puncture wound on the cheek is to be forensically examined. If it is found that it is a bullet-entry wound, then it gives credence to the theory that killer had killed them, and hacked off the heads to hide the calibre and details of the gun that was used. Port authorities said that the tide, and the speed of the river flow, were such that the head could not have floated down the Hunter River. It must have been carried to Newcastle by the killer.

The next day, forensics found that the small hole in Mrs Shelley's head was indeed made by bullets entering. Those bullets were extracted, and found to be from the same gun that killed her husband.

On the Tuesday, in Maitland Court, the police charged a Mr Terrence O'Connor with the double murder. He denied the charge. The police alleged, in a statement, that O'Connor and another man had planned to rob a pub in Newcastle. To do this they needed a gun, and it became known that Shelley had one. They went to Shelley's house, and stole a .32 calibre pistol from him. After the murders were discovered, the two defendants drove a utility to Newcastle, and threw the gun into the sea at a point he had indicated to the police.

O'Connor's solicitor said that the facts as stated were substantially correct, as far as it had gone. But he pointed out that there had been no mention of the killings in the statement, and that the accused denied having anything at all to do with the killings.

Mr O'Connor was remanded in custody until mid June. We will take up the story again at that date.

Comment. Feel sorry for Mrs Gladys Fleming, not only for the loss of the couple. But also she was required to identify her daughter by going to Newcastle to examine the floating head.

A FOOTNOTE ON CHILD CUSTODY

Letters, Rev D Wilcox. The tragedy at East Maitland in which a little child was deprived of both parents at once, most unexpectedly, should emphasise to all parents the great responsibility that is theirs to see that they make suitable provision for the guardianship of their children in the event of the children being left as orphans by any cause whatever.

There is an old myth which should be disposed of without delay to the effect that godparents would assume control of such children, until they reach 21 years, without any other legal provisions being made. This is completely contrary to the law in NSW.

As in this case, the Minister for Child Welfare automatically becomes the guardian of all such children for whom the parents have made no written provision in a will and he can use his own discretion entirely a to the manner in which he discharges his responsibilities. Grandparents, as such, cannot claim the right to bring up such children; they must be approved by the Child Welfare Department which will use its own methods to determine whether or not it regards such grandparents, or anyone else, as being suitable people to care for the children up to the age of 21 years.

On every occasion when I carry out a baptism, I point out to the parents that they should provide full legal protection for their children as they desire, by nominating guardians in a will so as to avoid later heartbreak in the event of the early death of both parents.

If this practice were more widely observed it would both help the children and make the task of the Child Welfare Department much easier.

ARREST OF ADOLF EICHMANN

Late in April, a small news item appeared on Page Three of most major newspapers. It told the story of the kidnap of Colonel Adolf Eichmann, somewhere overseas, and of his compulsory shipment to Israel, where he would be held in a gaol, and tried soon for war crimes. Over the next few days, more details emerged.

David Ben-Gurion, the Premier of Israel made an initial statement. He described Eichmann as "one of the greatest of the Nazi war criminals" who was responsible, together with the Nazi leaders, was for what they called the "final solution". That is, for the extermination of six million Jews. He has been found and captured by the Israel security services." Other statements revealed that those security forces had been constantly on the trail of Eichmann for the entire 15 years since the end of the War and had at last seized the opportunity to kidnap him a few days ago. There was a lot of speculation about where he was when he was seized, and commentators thought it most likely that he had been in Kuwait at the time.

Over the next few days, this story got some legs. In an official Israeli document he said, "I have been living all this time under terrible tension, and now, I am reconciled to my fate. I was not particularly surprised when it happened.

I had known all the time that something like this must happen in the end."

The people of Israel were not so sanguine. His capture had inflamed memories of war-time atrocities, and feeling was intense. One Russian store keeper said "torture him in lifelong solitary confinement by making him read endless reports on the six million who died." A student said "get some medieval laws still in existence. I wish to be present at his hanging." An Egyptian waiter had a simple solution "throw him to the dogs".

The London *Times* was characteristically more moderate, and knew a few more of the facts. "He began with the rank of sergeant working at Gestapo headquarters, and he was responsible for the expulsion of Jews from Austria. He was put in charge of the so-called Central Gestapo when the two offices were merged. This was a small office, and Eichmann never rose above the rank of lieutenant-colonel. His connection with the massacres in Poland and Russia was remote. The number of murders in which Eichmann had a direct hand is less than one million".

Comment. Only "less than a million." Sounds trivial to me. Give the guy a break.

Here in Australia, initial interest in this was muted. To most people it came as something of a surprise that, fifteen years after the War ended, the Israelis were still chasing War criminals so doggedly and professionally. But the main comments were on side issues, exemplified by this letter.

Letters, Stewart Moyser. The State of Israel now holds Adolf Eichmann captive and alleges that he was responsible for the death of millions of members of the Jewish faith during World War II.

These charges relate to monstrous crimes, and I can sympathise with the Jewish grief and understand the desire for revenge, but many other people who were not Jews died in World War II, some, possibly, on Eichmann's orders. The Israeli authorities should remember this when preparing their case and charge him with murder, irrespective of the religion of his victims.

If Israel charges Eichmann with have ordered the death of only Jews it will be maintaining the terms of the Nazi doctrine – that Jews are different from other people. It will appear to be interested in punishing only those who commit crimes against Jews. If Eichmann is found guilty, as Press reports indicate is likely, the charges, trial and sentence will be revenge, cloaked in legal forms.

Another point concerns me. What authority does the State of Israel have to try a man for offences committed outside its jurisdiction long before it was formed?

Will this case become a precedent for the abduction of anti-Semites from New York, or Sydney, for crimes against Jews that have gone unpunished?

The Allied War Crimes Tribunal of Nuremberg is disbanded but, if Germany maintains Courts for dealing with war crimes, he should be returned to them. The crimes were committed in German territory, not Israel.

So far, to the end of May, these events were buried on Page Three of the papers. In future months, as we shall see, they got quite accustomed to Page One.

OZ ABORIGINES

Letters, David Russell, Tokyo, Japan. The Herald recently reported the opening of a swimming-pool at Moree for Aborigines banned from the local public baths.

It was claimed that by attending the opening, various dignitaries were not approving **segregation**, and that in truth this was not segregation but that the pool was built because ill-health among the aborigines barred them from the public baths. Surely the answer is to remedy the cause. In this regard the avowed council policy could be sidestepped by the provision of more adequate medical services.

I am trying to advertise Australia and its way of life while in Asia on a program to improve international relations by personal contact, and I find it quite difficult enough to explain the barrier we have to Asian immigration without having to admit that Australians don't seem to be able to live with the few coloured people it has.

BLACKS ARE DIFFERENT?

Letters, J Somons, University of Sydney. A speaker on "the Nation's Forum of the Air", made an extraordinary statement to the effect that the blacks of South Africa are a different sort of being from the whites because "if a black receives a severe burn, skin cannot be grafted to replace the destroyed tissue." This argument was used to support the argument that blacks are incapable of running a parliamentary democracy.

We would point out that the statement is arrant nonsense and shows a complete ignorance of the findings of genetics and immunology.

To get the record straight, the success of skin grafting and organ transplantation has nothing to do with race, but depends upon factors within the individual. Grafts from one individual to another of all species are completely successful only in the case of identical twins of embryos.

COLOUR BLINDNESS

Letters, L Szego. A great number of potentially good drivers are debarred from obtaining a driver's licence because of colour blindness. This is quite unnecessary, and I would suggest that a start be made to rectify the position.

As the main reason for banning these people is their inability to distinguish the green "go" light from the red "stop" at traffic lights, let us paint a dark green "G" and a dark red "S" on the inside of each coloured glass. If necessary, also let us regulate the shape of rear lights on cars.

JUNE: BABES IN DAD'S ARMS

This month a young man, Edward Baliol, had a unique experience for an Australian man. He was allowed into the delivery room while his wife had a baby. He wrote a 20 column-inch report of the event for the Sydney Morning Herald. The tone of the article was one of wonderment, and of admiration for his wife, and he was clearly enamoured of the singular privilege that was granted him. A few paragraphs show his enthusiasm for the concept of allowing other men into what was strictly forbidden territory.

If you have ever seen a women in labour, you will understand. If you have seen your wife in labour, you will remember the intense joy and humility you felt. Such a shared joy can provide a lifelong bond between young married people, a bond not easily forgotten in the difficult years of marriage later on..... The child's head was clearly visible.

I stepped back, watched, waited; my breath imprisoned in my lungs. It seemed only minutes later that our slippery, squawking, daughter wriggled alive before our very eyes. Soon the tiny creature was placed in my wife's arms...... If you want to feel glad to be alive, see a mother with a minute-old child in her arms.....

There were lots of different opinions on whether such experiences should be shared.

Letters, J Barnard. Your comment at the start that it is a controversial question is encouraging, as my personal experience of Sydney hospitals and Sydney doctors has made me feel that there is no controversy, it being accepted that fathers must be barred from this experience with their wives.

Last year my wife and I thought it would be wonderful if I could be present at the birth of our child. Unfortunately, the powers-that-be decided that I could only be present at the "first stage" and, though this proved to be considerable help to my wife, it seemed wrong that I should be sent away. Mr Baliol is a very lucky man. I am sure that the hospital he mentioned must be in Melbourne, where this practice is more accepted.

Finally, I should add another reason to be there. He would be able to witness any acts of callous and sadistic behaviour to the mother by the nursing staff, which unfortunately happens at certain hospitals and causes considerable mental scarring.

Letters, G Cowlishaw. I must warn your pregnant mothers to make sure that they choose their hospitals well. At one large city hospital, women are treated as ignorant, hysterical creatures. Solitary confinement is used effectively to destroy confidence when a woman is most vulnerable. Questions and conversation meet with patronising smiles rather than helpful information.

Why are doctors and hospital authorities not educated in the modern attitude to childbirth, proved to be most effective. Have they the right to deny married couples the experience of Mr Baliol.

Letters, Mrs R Desmond. With regard to the article "I Saw My Son Born" by Mr Baliol and the letter from J Barnard it seems that both these fathers take it for granted that all wives wish their husbands to be present during childbirth, and also that all fathers wish to be present. I can assure them that in the great majority of cases this is not so.

When my two sons were born, I had no desire whatsoever for my husband to be present to distract me in any way from the tremendous physical exertion on hand, and friends I have spoken to on the subject are of the same opinion.

I might add that our husbands' only thoughts were to get us out of the way and safely in hospital as soon as they could!

Letters, Audley Green. I should like to point out to Mrs R Desmond that no one has suggested that it be made compulsory for the husband to be present at the confinement; there are no doubt as many wives who would prefer their husbands to be elsewhere as there are husbands whose presence would be of no help to their wives.

Dr Grantly Read insists that if the husband and wife wish to be together, the husband should be both an emotionally stable person and familiar with the sequence of events in the birth process. It should be the doctor's right to decide whether the husband is the type of person who will help his wife during labour, and whether he should be present.

My husband and I wanted very much to be together for the whole of my confinement. We talked to

my doctor, who said the hospital would not allow
it. On two occasions we took our request to the
hospital, only to be told: "We don't allow that kind
of thing here", as though we had wanted something
decidedly improper!

Letters, Wendy Smith. I find it hard to believe
that any husband could achieve such a welter of
ego-based emotions merely from watching his wife
perpetrate the rather messy "miracle" of giving
birth.

Surely Mr Baliol and all those others who are
so anxious to share his "experience" must be
motivated, at least to some extent, by curiosity?

Speaking as a physiotherapist, much of whose
time on duty has been spent in pre- and post-
maternity work, I have met few, indeed very few,
women who expressed any wish to have their
husbands around at any stage of labour. Indeed,
quite the contrary would be true. Most mothers,
and I am one, appreciate the privacy and efficiency
to be found in our "father-free" labour wards.

Let the fathers save their feelings of pride, humility
and love for when mum brings junior home.
Perhaps then they may be inspired to help her
with some with the laundry, which would be far
more practical, I feel, than holding her hand in the
labour ward!

Comment. Obviously, opinions were divided. When I was
writing my **1948 book**, the same question was raised. As
far as I can see there had been little change in the conduct of

hospitals and doctors, and no change in how the population felt about the way it all was being handled.

My own experience, with one of my children, was at Kurri Kurri hospital, 120 miles north of Sydney. There the matron happened to be at the front desk as we checked in at 5 p.m. on a Friday afternoon. She took over immediately, then told me "leave now and come back at 10 on Sunday morning. And don't ring. We are short staffed." This was hard on the family, but even harder on my wife. She gave birth at five o'clock the next morning, and was incommunicado till ten the next day. In practice, it worked out a bit better. My sister was a Teaching Sister at nearby Cessnock Hospital, and we were able to set up communications. But it was still a long wait until my wife and baby were brought out next morning by the now-charming and triumphant matron, very keen to be part of the goodwill that abounded at that moment.

I think at times about these and other bullies. There were plenty of them round in those days. I resented matrons and Sisters, bank managers and clerks, station managers and station staff, and Post Masters. I found police of all ranks very friendly and relaxed, that staff at counters were good, and shopkeepers were a bundle of fun. I suppose everyone had their own likes and dislikes. But one thing that is true is that people **now** are much more ready to fire back than they were 50 years ago. If, for example, a matron pulled some modern-day caper on people today, the reaction of most people would be much more vigorous than mine was a long time ago.

WHITE VERSUS BLACK? COMING TO YOU?

The Blacks of Africa were now in a continent-wide fight for independence. In South Africa, the Whites had tried to guide this movement in many ways, but in the long run, suppression had won out. But there were other scenarios developing at this very time. The worst case was in the Congo. There Belgium, the colonial power, had resolved a few years ago to leave as gracefully as possible, and had made as much preparation as it could in a time frame that was too short. But it set up some instruments of democracy, and held elections, all of which in the first instant, seemed to go well.

But within a week, the Blacks had taken to the streets and were menacing and attacking and killing the Whites and their families and destroying their property, the US Navy was evacuating Americans under emergency conditions, the Belgian Army had sent thousands of troops, and Russia was doing what it could to stir up as much trouble as possible. At the same time, two Congolese States decided they wanted to be completely free from anyone, and tried to withdraw. They formed their own armies, and went to battle with the central government. At this exact time, similar situations were developing in Southern Rhodesia and Kenya.

This letter below gives a good idea of the widespread trouble.

Letters, R Embleton-Smith, Sydney. Having recently arrived from South Africa, I was rather shaken to read the sweeping statements from Rev Pocklington in your Letters. He attributes the recent Congolese atrocities to (1) a lack of kindness of the part of the whites, and (2) an alleged habit of Europeans of ravishing the native female population. He also inferred that no doubt the natives of South Africa, given the chance, would "get their own back" the same way.

I can assure Mr Pocklinton, at least on the part of the majority of South Africans, that kindness is not lacking in that country; nor are the Belgian people noted for any lack of culture. It is time that people overseas stopped looking upon the white peoples of Africa as a race of oppressors. They are, of course, ordinary decent people, such as you find the world over. My many South African friends spend a large part of their lives trying to understand the natives and give them a square deal. Often their reward is loyalty; frequently it is petty deceit, theft, ingratitude or just plain apathy. To suggest that they exploit them and "ravish" them is far-fetched, to put it mildly.

In southern Africa (and, I confidently expect, in the Congo) the white countryman lives in no fear of the tribal native. It is in the towns, whither natives are attracted and cut off from tribal organisation, that the trouble begins. Freed from tribal laws, the native casts off all moral restraints; marriage is almost unknown and few children know their fathers; the native townships are ruled by gangs of thugs who terrorise their neighbours and extort "protection money" from them. A visit to Baragwanath Hospital, on a Sunday evening would open Mr Pocklington's eyes. There he would see dozens of natives dying of stab wounds and cracked skulls – inflicted, I hasten to add, by their fellow Africans and not by the white population. Their ideas of right and wrong are primitive indeed.

It took about 1,900 years to bring democracy and justice to England. Where the Belgian Government seems to have erred is in imagining, like Mr Pocklington, that 100 years of white rule is enough to turn primitive tribes into civilised human beings, fit to take their place in the great councils of the world.

Australians, try as we might, could not ignore the ceaseless news of battle coming out of Africa. We felt at this time that we had already settled the race issue with our Aborigines in this far-sighted nation, and that we were not to get involved. On the other hand, so insistent was the bad news that some forward thinkers were worrying about New Guinea. Granted this land of 26 million people as a nation was miles behind Africa in its quest for independence, but this clearly would not last, and in fact, with the African examples it was certain to come to some decision point sooner now than later.

Letters, R Robson. It is inevitable that recent events in the Congo will be used as propaganda by the South African Government to justify its own repressive policies. Exactly the opposite lesson must be learnt by a country such as Australia, confronted as we are by a native problem in New Guinea.

Our deepest sympathies must be extended to the Belgian settlers who have been passing through the most ghastly ordeal, but we must ask ourselves why the transfer of authority in the Congo generated an explosion of the most hideous racial violence accompanied by a reversion by many natives to forms of barbarism. Compare this with the orderly transfer of power upon the granting of independence by Great Britain to her former colonies in Africa and Asia.

There will surely be no finer chapter in the history of the British Empire than the wonderful manner in which the colonial peoples were steadily prepared to eventual self-government. The British Administrations and settlers did more than build harbours, roads, railways, mines and cities. Side by side with the development and opening up of the country they built schools and universities and they trained doctors, lawyers, engineers and Civil servants.

In recent years, the Belgians appear to have adopted a more enlightened policy in the Congo, but it has obviously been impossible to eradicate the lingering memories of the old Congo Free State which was run as the personal empire of King Leopold with the most brutal forms of slavery and oppression of the natives. As yet in New Guinea no awareness of nationalism has manifested itself among the natives but, despite the multiplicity of races and languages and the backwardness of the people, this will surely come.

In the meantime, to retain any goodwill and influence in New Guinea in years to come, Australia must press forward with a far more ambitious program to speed up the educational, political and social development of the New Guinea peoples. We must remember that less than a year ago Belgians with long experience in the Congo were saying that it would be many years before the Congolese were ready for even the most elementary forms of self-government.

Bob Menzies was just starting to see the writing on the wall. He issued a statement late in June saying that we should not expect to be custodians of the New Guinea population for more than thirty years. This might sound a long time in the future, but it was much earlier than ever proposed before. It was heralded by some as "a change in policy." Arthur Calwell, the Labor leader, went off for two weeks to New Guinea to "see things" first-hand, and he even did a "jig" with some native tribesman. But when he returned he stated that there was **no hope of independence in "thirty, or even forty years."** Arthur had not seen any writing on any wall anywhere in New Guinea.

MORE ON ADOLF EICKMANN

Feelings on Eichmann were muted early in June. There were many Jews, and others, who were vitally interested in what happened, but up till now, the affair had been so cloak-and dagger by the Israelis that no one felt they had anything to go on. At the most, there were a few people who registered a plea for balanced justice, and not lynch mobs.

Letters, Stewart Moyser. My concern over the Eichmann case is not for Eichmann. Not for any other anti-Semites. It is that the desire to punish him should not damage established legal procedures, because these are safeguards for all men.

All Australians have an expectation that he should be tried correctly. If he is not, our concepts of justice will suffer, not Eichmann.

But on June 3rd, the veil of secrecy was lifted a little. Argentina asked Israel for full details of the Eichmann capture, to determine whether Israel had taken him from within the nation of Argentina, in violation of international law. It was stated by informants that agents had in fact seized him in Argentina in May, and they had taken him to Israel. It was stated that one evening he stepped off a bus in the early evening to walk home, where his German-born wife and four children were waiting for him. The Israelis dashed up in a car and bundled him in. Six hours later he was in a plane leaving going from Tel Aviv.

This news was startling to the world. Did this mean that agents from one nation were free to "invade " another, and on their own evidence, kidnap a person legitimately there? Put this together with the Gary Powers spy plane incident over Russia, and his spying on a foreign country, and the question became whether the sovereignty of any persons in any nation was guaranteed.

We will look to see what answers emerged to this question over the next few months.

ANIMAL ACTS

Antoine, the 22 year-old lion trainer at Bullen Brothers' Circus, has some good days, and some bad ones. Two months ago, he was "chewed about" by a bear, and spent

14 days in hospital. Then yesterday, he had an experience more suited to his august profession.

He was having a quiet day at the office, so to speak, "working" his five tigers in a cage at Bathurst in front of a crowd of 1,800 people. Suddenly, Queenie, who was "spoiled rather than dangerous" decided a pounce was in order, and acted accordingly. "She had me down in the sawdust in a flash. She opened her mouth wide to take a bite at my head."

So, and you doubtless know this, Antoine used an "old lion-trainers' trick. "I clenched my left fist, and drove it down her throat. It made her choke. Tigers can't close their jaws with a fist down their throat."

At this stage, Antoine was still sharing the ground with the sawdust, and the tiger was standing over him, still interested in an early supper. However, tragedy (for Antoine, but not the tiger) was averted by Kevin Bullen running into the cage, and driving the spoilt Queenie off with a chair. Antoine, bleeding from claw rips to both shoulders, and arms and legs, finished the act, before receiving medical treatment. He said later that "it is all part of the job", and shrugged his lacerated shoulders. He added "the show must go on."

Comment. Some of you will remember Bullen's and Wirth's Circuses, and others. They are different in many ways from those of today, not the least because they had lions and tigers, and elephants, and monkeys and gorillas, and snakes. It made for some wonderful entertainment, where the crowd sat round and hoped that some Queenie would act spoilt, and maul a trainer, and yet were horrified by the prospect. It appears as if those days are gone for good. Although some say they are gone for the worse.

Letters, Crystal Rrogers, Chairman, "The Animals Friend", Delhi, India. I wish to draw the attention of your readers to the decision of the Pakistan Government to export the country's stray dogs to Korea to be slaughtered for soup.

Apart from the unspeakable suffering that the animals will have to endure during transit, there is also the health aspect. Few stray dogs in the east are healthy specimens, and in being used for human consumption, it is impossible to estimate what diseases may not be spread to human beings.

The only thing that might avert this evil is world censure, and I would beg all those who read this, and particularly animal-lovers, to make this matter known wherever possible, in order that such a storm of protest may be raised from all over the world that the Pakistani Government may be dissuaded from carrying out its plan.

Letters, B Wilson. These hypocritical dog-lovers prattle about being animal-lovers, but overlook the fact that horses and other animals have to be killed to feed dogs. Why not admit they are dog-lovers just because a dog flatters all human failings and vices with his servile fawnings and goes gladly and willingly along with man in man's most cruel and inhumane activities.

How about horses and cows? Horses serve man faithfully with real help and are then killed for dog food; and cows give milk from which we derive many life-sustaining products, but no one hesitates in killing a cow once her usefulness is over. And sheep are the most inoffensive and mild of animals and would probably make better pets than dogs, yet they are cruelly slaughtered without a crocodile tear.

If these hypocrites were real animal-lovers, they wouldn't eat meat themselves or keep a dog.

CIVIL DEFENCE SPENDING

Letters, Senator J Ormonde. The news that Departmental Estimates may be cut is alarming if this is to apply to civil defence. Despite all the talk of nuclear missile warfare, it should be of interest to the public to know that in 1959-60, the amount voted for civil defence in Australia by the Commonwealth Government was 300,000 Pounds. Of that sum, 200,000 Pounds was returned to the Treasury, unspent. That works out at two and a half pence per head of population.

It could be that Mr Menzies has no fear that Australia is in any danger from outside attack. He may also feel that it is wasting public funds to spend money on civil defence. If this is so, he should take the public into his confidence.

JULY: GRAEME THORNE KIDNAPPED

On the morning of Thursday, July 8, a young boy called Graeme Thorn set off for his school, affluent Scots College, in Sydney's Eastern suburbs. He was a good natured, happy child, well liked by his mates, and distinguished from them only by the fact that his father had won a large lottery in the recent past. He was to picked up on the way by a woman family friend in the normal manner.

A few hours into the school day, Mrs Thorne received a phone call from a man with apparently a foreign accent. He told her he had taken the boy, and that the family would have to pay 15,000 Pounds if they wanted his release. Mrs Thorne, distraught, contacted the police to report this kidnapping, and a man-hunt for the boy was immediately started. His father, on his way down from Kempsey, was told of the crime and of his loss, and he made a dramatic radio and television call to the criminal to release the boy.

For days and weeks, the police search went on. Huge resources were thrown into scouring the area, the public was universally anxious and willing to help, every lead was followed up meticulously. A day later, Graeme's school case, with his name printed in gold letters on it, was found just off the road on the Wakehurst Park Highway out near Dee Wye.

There were reports of him being held on a boat on the Hawkesbury River. Hundreds of reports came in and were investigated and nothing of value was found. Some of his clothes were later found, and the question was whether this indicated he might be nearby, or whether they were planted to fool the police. Sadly, no one knew.

A reward of 5,000 Pounds was offered for information, by the NSW Government, and another 10,000 Pounds by the Herald newspapers. The Police Commissioner and the Lord Mayor of Sydney each made public appeals to the kidnapper or kidnappers to release the boy and promised that they would be granted immunity from prosecution if the lad was unharmed. All this effort, and genuine concern from the whole Australian community, was to no avail.

Australia was shocked. The comment made was that **we do not have this type of crime in Australia.** Everyone knew about kidnappings and ransom demands in America, and in other places. But **"we do not have that type of crime here"** was said over and over again. It was the shattering of a fantasy, of a belief that somehow we were protected from the worst of the world's woes.

We could accept somewhat the idea that men like Gary Powers would spy on us, and that Israeli agents might swoop on a supposed war criminal in our midst. But there was no way we could believe that an innocent schoolboy would be taken from his parents and held to ransom. The very idea of it shook the nation to the core, and confronted everyone with the realisation of how vulnerable we were, and are.

Letters to the newspapers.   This sample below shows the range of emotions that were evoked. Some writers are angry, laying blame, some are legalistic, and some are prayerful. But each of them express some of the **one**

feeling that gripped **all** Australians, the feeling of utterly frustrated helpless disbelief.

Letters, R Anderson. The safety of Graeme Thorne, as well as of other children, can best be assured by swift Government action. A law should be passed immediately, to come into effect after three days, imposing either the death penalty or life imprisonment plus a flogging, for either kidnapping any person for ransom or detaining any person kidnapped before that date.

This would leave the kidnappers a chance of escaping liability for the heavier penalty by releasing the child within those three days, while bringing them within its scope if they did not. They should realise, too, that his release would reduce the intensity of the efforts which the public must otherwise keep up to capture them, and give them more chance of escaping the present penalties.

Letters, A Citizen. Only very few people have been able to offer help in the form of clues in the Graeme Thorne kidnapping case. May I suggest that we can all help, not only in joining in the prayers offered in churches on Sundays, but also in offering prayers during the daily round throughout the week? And not only should we ask for the safe return of Graeme; we should pray also for the comfort of his parents and the guidance of those in charge of the case and for a change of heart of the kidnappers.

"More things are wrought by prayer than this world dreams of."

Letters, CIVIS. I have been greatly disturbed by the attitude of the Commissioner of Police and of the Lord Mayor in inviting the kidnapper of Graeme Thorne to deliver up the boy on terms that ransom money will be paid, and that the identity of the kidnapper will not be disclosed.

This is an open invitation to any blackguard to commit this foul crime and get away with it free of any consequences. There is no knowing what irreparable harm might be done by such a course.

Nobody can fail to have the deepest sympathy with the parents, but as the kidnapper has refused all appeals, and so much time has elapsed, it would seem to me that no harm is likely to come to the boy if such promises were immediately withdrawn, as they ought to be.

Letters, M Rathbone. In reference to Graeme Thorne, the Premier, Mr Heffron said, "Somehow we have never thought that kidnapping a child and holding him to ransom could occur in this country."

Yet thousands of TV viewers saw a BBC film on Channel 2 two days before the event, which dealt with the kidnapping of two young girls whose father had won a similar prize.

So this kidnapping immediately points out two morals. One is that crime films teach crime, and the other is that extravagant gambling with fabulously high prizes invariably brings disaster.

Letters, Michael Thornhill. No doubt the police will realise their indebtedness to Mr Rathbone for his important lead in the kidnapping mystery, and may even consider his right to a substantial part of the reward.

Assuming, with your correspondent, that the culprit was taught the crime by ABN's "Dial 999" last Monday night, it follows that he had two days to discover Mr Thorne's identity and address; that he had two mornings to discover that Graeme was in fact Mr Thorne's son and nobody else's, and that he had two mornings to discover the boy's habits on the way to school and so to plan the kidnapping.

To learn all these details in such a short time is a tall order indeed. So we may assume that some of them at least were known before watching "Dial 999." It now follows that he was somehow acquainted with Graeme or Mr Thorne; thus he is either a friend of the Thornes, or a local resident.

We further know that the criminal was one of the one-twentieth of Sydney's population who watch "Dial 999". An investigation of the few suspects left would solve mystery.

Naturally, your correspondent will not regard this as a reductio ad absurdum of his explanation of the coincidence. He will probably continue to believe, unsupported, what he wishes to believe. That is, that crime films teach crime.

Letters, Bessie Donegani. I would like to suggest to authorities that in future the names of winners of major prizes in lotteries and Art Unions should be withheld. The winning numbers could be published.

Holders of winning tickets could be notified by post, and so protected from this new development in our Australian way of life, and also from the indignity of begging letters.

Letters, R Power. The recent kidnapping has shocked our community and responsible persons have suggested that the maximum penalty should be attached to this crime, and that it should be made retrospective to cover the present case.

While I agree that kidnapping should be made a crime with a heavy penalty, I feel that life imprisonment should not be made the penalty. After all, a kidnapper would be tempted to kill his victim because the punishment could be no heavier, and he would have reduced the chance of being caught

The principle of retrospectively changing laws negates all of our ideas of justice. In our community each citizen knows, or can find out, just where he stands in relation to the law and to alter this would destroy putting faith in our judicial system.

Therefore, while the community has every sympathy with those affected by the current case, its lawmakers should not allow a wave of hysteria to influence their judgement, and should consider closely before establishing new legal systems and judgements.

WHAT'S HAPPENING TO MIGRANTS?

The Minister for Immigration, Mr A Downer, said that the number of migrants from Europe was increasing, and that would certainly diminish our ties with Britain. He thought that the current level of British migrants, 65,000 per year, was as good as we would be able to get, and that about the same number would come from Europe in the future.

He said that some people might be concerned by this trend, and he urged them not to worry. European migrants were being readily assimilated here, and their inclusion into our society was adding to our national diversity, encouraging our national independence and self sufficiency. It also helped us to foster an attitude that was less parochial and that in turn helped us to be heard in world councils.

Letters, Sandor Berger.   I am a Hungarian-born Australian who landed here 11 years ago. I feel it is time for me to draw the attention of those native-born Australians who talk about lack of willingness on the part of newcomers to assimilate themselves and become naturalised.

One thing that is obvious is that every time I show any sign of disagreement with Australia, I get "Why don't you go back where you came from?" Then there are other more subtle attacks like "How long have you been here?" and "Of course, you are a Hungarian, aren't you?"

I don't think we should be asked to go more than half-way to meet those who only advance a half-hearted and, in many cases, reluctant step or two towards us. After all, even though our former lives have been uprooted, we still have some dignity left.

Most of us newcomers desire to assimilate ourselves fully into the Australian way of life, and are willing to go halfway and wait there with outstretched hands. But we are not sycophantic crawlers, and I do not really believe any intelligent Australian would want us to be.

DEATH OF COUNTRY TOWNS

Letters, Prof D Orchard, Highway Engineering, Uni of NSW. One major aspect of our national development and planning, which is in reverse gear, is the slow dying of most country towns. They are becoming ghosts of their former healthy, prosperous selves.

If you made a survey of the country towns of NSW, you would find a few of the larger ones developing, mainly at the expense of their small unfortunate neighbours.

But the small are fighting a war which they can't win. Industries close, families move out, builders leave, big and small stores and other types of businesses find turnover below the economic level and many fold up.

Among those who care there is a feeling of pessimism and despair, because these retrograde steps mean reduced educational facilities.

Letters, H Grosch. The factors mentioned as causing the drift of people from country to city omit the major cause – farm mechanisation.

The wool and wheat farmer can now work, with mechanisation, about 1,000 acres single-handed, whereas before mechanisation at least three workers were required for a similar acreage. These people all lived on the farm or in the nearby township or village. With the loss of employment through mechanisation the farm worker has progressively drifted off to the city. The consequent decline of population has been reflected in the derelict condition of many small townships and rural villages.

An extension of the drift trend is seen in the latter-day development where the farmer and his family live in town, where schooling and amenities are easier to come by. Travel to and from the farm is no different from, and probably easier than, the city equivalent of daily travel to and from work.

The larger towns feel the effects of the population drift also, and this is reflected in reiterated claims for the establishment of rural town industries. However, farm mechanisation and population drift may be considered evolutionary trends unlikely to be affected by comparatively minor developments such as the transfer of some industries to some towns.

Competent appraisement of local population trends, with planned stabilisation of local business based on local population, is sorely needed.

LET'S HAVE A WHIP ROUND

Let's have a whip-around. A Council meeting was held in the NSW country city of Nyngan last night. Recently, such meetings had been very lively, with many Councillors showing their wisdom and expressing their democratic rights by dramatically walking out of meetings. The Mayor, Mr Wren, himself had previously walked out of four since he was elected ten months earlier.

This particular meeting was considered worth watching because a Mr Campbell, the editor of the local "Observer", was considered likely to address the Chair from the floor, which as everyone knows, was strictly taboo. Mr Campbell had earned the wrath of Mr Wren because he had published a story about the removal of a refrigerator from a ratepayer's house in defiance of his orders. A crowd of about thirty ratepayers was present to witness any fireworks.

Halfway through the meeting, Mr Campbell started interrupting. The floor would not give him permission to speak. He persisted. Still no permission. Then Mr Wren could stand it no longer. He rose from his seat, grabbed hold of a 3-foot long leather whip from beside his seat, and with loud threatening exclamations, indicated a strong desire to horsewhip the errant editor.

Fortunately for Mr Campbell, he was restrained, and Mr Wren soon calmed down. He explained "I happened to buy a whip today because of wild dogs at my home, and on the spur of the moment I took hold of the whip, and went to whip him out of the Chamber." He said that next meeting he would have police present, and they could remove any persistent interjectors. The crowd in the gallery left obviously disappointed that there was no whipping.

Not surprisingly, this all occurred in Bogan Shire.

GROWING ACCEPTANCE OF JAPAN

Fifteen years after the end of the Japanese War, many people were beginning to re-assess their hatred of the Japanese. Trade between the two nations has started up again, our troops had spent many years there as an Occupation force, and indeed there were many children of mixed races that had been born out of that Occupation. No one was likely to forget, but the population was **starting** to forgive.

But, I enclose the following Letter as a reminder that not everyone felt so generous.

Letters, N Lloyd. The Japanese are against the proposed US-Japan Peace Treaty because it would mean the occupation of their country for another 11 years. They should have thought about that when they attacked America. If they had won the War, America and Australia would have been occupied forever. I propose that that is exactly what we should do to their country.

MAYBE TRY SAFETY BELTS?

Letters, J Wright. From pictures and reports of the tragic accident which caused the death of one of our most eminent and highly esteemed citizens, Mr Samuel Hordern, I notice that the rear compartment of the car was comparatively undamaged and that the injuries were caused by the passengers being thrown from their seats. One cannot help but wonder whether this tragedy would have been avoided had **safety belts been worn**.

BOB AND DOLLY DYER

This energetic and talented couple were about to launch a new version of their popular Pick-a-Box quiz show. Bob promised that the show would be bigger and brighter than ever before.

To Pick-a-Box, all you need to do is go to your BP service station and pick up an entry ticket. Fill it in, and include a number from 1 to 40. Cards will be entered in a raffle, and the drawn card will win a prize corresponding to the number on the ticket. This could be a car, a cruise to America, air holidays, furs and household appliances.

US ELECTIONS LOOMING

The Americans had just picked their candidates for the position of President in the election coming up in November. For the Republican side was the youthful Richard Nixon.

There was also the Democrat candidate, John Kennedy. The charismatic Senator was trying to move up a notch, from his previous job of Senator. He and and his attractive wife were wooing voters with their beauty and charm.

WOMEN ON JURIES

Letters, Mrs S Campbell. Men have been trying to keep women out of everything for centuries. One of their methods is a benign and patronising attitude that women are inferior. For centuries women have been nodding their heads and agreeing, knowing full well that this is not so and that they are, at the very least, quite equal to any male.

All over the world they are quietly proving this and men, bless their little hearts, are absolutely terrified. They wave their arms and shout that women are too emotional, inconsistent, biased (towards what they don't explain) and completely lacking in everything that makes a Man.

But they must surely have their backs to the wall when they use the lack of toilet facilities at a courthouse as a means to keep women from serving on a jury. If any woman is public-spirited and courageous enough to have reached as far as actually serving, then I'm quite sure she won't let a small matter of toilet facilities defeat her.

Letters, S Sack. Campbell's whining Letter misses most of the important points. Firstly, her assertion that men keep women out. They do sometimes. They keep them out of pits, out of working in gangs on the railway, out of working on the streets in all kinds of weather.

They keep them from mustering cattle, from fighting wars, from working overtime, from being killed on building sites, from chemical poisoning on the job, from sticking out all sorts of difficult situations when it gets tough. I could go on and on, but I am not a whinging woman so I know when to stop.

About toilets for women jurors. Campbell would obviously be the first to whinge if the toilets provided were not adequate. I have worked in the Court system from many years, and I can tell you that none of the toilets for jurors, or for employees, are adequate. In fact, they stink.

If the dear lady ever got near them she would have the horrors. Again, I will not go on about them. But to propose that they somehow be shared with the ladies who would become jurors is silly. They would be affronted, and then we would have another bunch of martyrs to listen to.

Could new facilities be built? Yes, they are being built. By men, with no women workers in sight to do the heavy work. Will they be adequate? Yes they will be adequate. They will be prim and proper and more than satisfy the desires of the dear ladies who will fix their makeup in them.

Will they be of the same standard as those provided for men? No they will not be. They will be of a much higher standard. Little works of art. Why not of the same standard? Because of the attitude of society, and Campbell, that men are dirty creatures, fit only for toil and bringing home money, and never ever capable of appreciating any finer things.

I welcome women jurors, but only if they have some sense. Campbell wants immediate gratification, and if she does not have the sense to realise that development of facilities takes a short time, then the jury system would be better off not having the benefit of her wisdom.

AUGUST: GRAEME THORNE'S BODY FOUND

Two young lads playing in bushland yesterday made the grim discovery of a partly decomposed body, wrapped in a brightly coloured blanket, in the undergrowth at the bottom of a rock outcrop near the seaside Sydney suburb of Seaforth. Police were called, and they confirmed that it was the body of Graeme Thorne.

Late last night, they were of the opinion that it had been there for several weeks and that he had probably died soon after the kidnapping. He was still clad in the school uniform from Scots College that he had been wearing when kidnapped. His hands and feet had been tied with a short length of cord. A doctor, who did a thorough examination, was not yet able to determine the cause of death, but there were no obvious bullet or stab wounds. The following day, a post mortem revealed that the boy had suffered a fractured skull, from a heavy instrument. It was now believed that he had been later strangled with the scarf that was found at the scene.

One of the main clues that the police had to work with was the rug that the lad had been wrapped in. The photo was circulated through the nation, and people were encouraged to come forward and identify such rugs and their owners. Police continued their wide manhunt for the killer or killers, and for a time, only the suffering of Grahame's family and friends made the. news.

Letter writers came out in force.

Letters, J Hassett. The public are aghast at the spate of horrible murders and other crimes of violence that have been committed in recent years. To mention only a few, the kidnapping and murder of a boy, the abduction of a girl from school and her subsequent rape and murder, the braining of two little boys with an axe, the decapitation of a man and his wife, and the murder of a policeman and his wife and child with a bomb.

This spate of violence is the result of the State Government abolishing capital punishment, whittling down life sentences to 20 years (and in some cases, to 14 and 12 years), putting dangerous criminals on comfortable prison farms instead of gaol, boasting about its policy of "restoring criminals to the community", and providing other incitements to crime.

It is the duty of all citizens to write to their members of Parliament demanding that this appeasement must cease, as it can only result in more and more atrocities, as did the appeasement of the Nazis by Chamberlain in 1938.

Comment. Poor Neville Chamberlain. How did he get into all this?

Letters, Jas McIntosh. We are being continually told, especially by the Police Commissioner, Mr Delaney, that we have the best police force in the world. The sooner that myth is exploded, the better. Sheer incompetence is glaringly obvious from top to bottom, particularly at the top, and it is my suggestion that the top 12 should be sacked at once.

With regard to the offer of a free pardon extended by the Government in the Thorne matter, I am firmly of the opinion that there should be no such offer made.

Surely any accomplice to such a foul and revolting crime such as this deserves the strongest possible punishment? Moreover, I believe it to be a duty to the community for the Government that such a person, if caught, should never be free to perpetuate or assist in a similar crime.

The Government should not overlook the element of chance which, together with the prayers of the nation, may eventually betray the culprit or culprits as the case may be.

Letters, G Lowenthal. On a first thought, the death penalty appears as an excellent deterrent. But opposition to it is not based on sentiment or frustration. It is based on long experience and careful study of all aspects of this experience. Those who have done this are all but unanimous in their complete denial of the usefulness of executions which are based on three things.

One. There is an undesirable effect on the executioner, and on the whole prison system. **Two**. Rather than promote justice, they promote sensationalism and other equally undesirable trends. **Three**. They are no deterrent, not least because murderers act either on impulse or in the expectation of evading capture.

Real deterrents are the certainty of detection and arrest, and a community feeling which uncompromisingly condemns all crime.

Letters, Chas Rochester. Experience in the United States has shown that kidnappers nearly always murder their victims to destroy vital evidence against themselves, and, no doubt, out of sheer viciousness. In the heat of police pursuits, kidnappers are not likely to stop and carefully calculate just how much punishment they will get if they murder their victim, and just how much they will get if they don't.

The best way to prevent combined kidnapping and murder is to provide the maximum deterrent against kidnapping in the first place, by capital punishment, or by life imprisonment (and not one day less) accompanied by flogging.

Comment on the outlook in 2010. This battle over capital punishment had been fought and re-fought often before and after the World War, and in many jurisdictions. No one ever seemed to change their mind, and the tendency towards leniency seemed always to continue to rise slowly.

But in the last few years, there have been signs (in 2009) that Governments will reverse the trends. For example, the suspension of Habeas Corpus so that terrorist suspects can be gaoled for 28 days without charge, and without access to lawyers and visitors. There are a few commentators today who argue that this is the start of a trend towards making punishment for major crimes tougher, and that this new toughness might extend in due course to murder and kidnapping. We will have to wait and see.

LIQUOR FOR ABORIGINES

On August 22, the NSW Chief Secretary, Mr Kelly, said he would urge the State Government to lift restrictions on the supply of liquor to Aborigines. The Aborigines' Welfare Board had recommended this, and he though it appropriate to do so.. He gave a number of reasons which included the fact that the restriction was based solely on race, and because the temperate drinker was being penalise because of the behaviour of the intemporates.

In any case, the present restraints were not stopping the supply of rubbish alcohol and methylated spirits to the Aborigines. He added that it was humiliating for many Aborigines whose moral standards were in no way inferior to many white persons.

Michael Sawtell was a longstanding member of Aborigines' Welfare Board of NSW, and was very familiar to readers of the *SMH* Letters for his vigorous statements on Aborigines. Invariably, when he wrote, about four times a year, he touched on matters that society considered sensitive, and opened up heated discussion.

Generally, he offended liberal-minded readers with his entrenched opposition to reform, and his refusal to grant most concessions. Yet his hard logic, and real knowledge of Aboriginal life, made him a hard man to gainsay.

In this case, the Board had suggested to the NSW Government that the law be changed so that Aborigines would be allowed to buy alcohol from a pub. At the moment, it was illegal for a publican to serve them. As you will see below, Sawtell opposed the relaxation of the law, and fired off his usual letter to the *SMH*. And as usual he got some good responses.

Letters, Micheal Sawtell, Member of the Aborigines' Welfare Board, Sydney. I have had a vast experience among all types of aborigines and I have been a Member of the Board for 17 years, so I think I know most of the facts concerning this most distressing problem.

I am irrevocably against lifting Section 9 from the Protection Act. The police representative on the Board, and also Mr S Wyatt, MLA, voted with me. I have great respect for the police; no one knows more or has more to do with Aborigines than they do. I am not advocating prohibition but protection. I wish to protect those backward persons of Aboriginal blood from indulging in the degradation of the white man.

Here is a point you do not seem to know. How about Aborigines buying drink in the town then taking it out to our stations? What a time our managers will have protecting the women and children from drunken Aborigines. It might be quite in order to allow Aborigines in Redfern in the city, but not for the whole State. With open go in blacks' camps such as Enngoonia and others out west, there will be murder every night. Lifting Section 9 is a cruel and evil suggestion.

Letters, J Horner. The enforcement of Section 9 prevents Aborigines from drinking with their white counterparts, and thus removes one way of welding the two races into one wholesome community.

Letters, H Spencer. I suggest that Mr Kelly pay a visit to some centre with a relatively high percentage of blacks in the population. Like Brewarina or Wilcannia. He should have a close look at the problem himself.

In the meantime he should consider how much actual time has been spent among the Aborigines by those who want to make the changes.

You have to live for a while in close proximity to these centres to fully appreciate the problem It is all very commendable to take the side of the Aborigines, and to thus encourage what they call assimilation, but there is something in the make-up of the Aborigine which will simply not permit of an intake of liquor that would be rated as moderate by a white man without causing a violent atavistic eruption.

Letters, L Fox. Replying to Michael Sawtell can be a somewhat monotonous business, but his latest claim, that the lifting of the liquor ban on Aborigines would lead to "murder every night", is just plain silly. Obviously Mr Sawtell has a vivid imagination. This is a valuable gift if kept in restraint. But facts are facts, and the experience of prohibition in America showed conclusively that prohibition does not lessen crime. In fact, it increases it. The reason is obvious, because prohibition does not prevent people from getting alcohol; it merely means that they get worse liquor at worse prices and drink it more rapidly (and often in greater quantities).

When prohibition is associated with race discrimination, the position is worsened. As a friend of mine put it the other day, "if the Japanese had taken this country and banned Australia from smoking, I'd have smoked myself to death in protest." And it is a fact that a number of Aborigines who drink to excess do so, partly at least, as a protest against the inferior status which the liquor ban imposes on them.

Letters, Walter Bass. Concerning Mr Sawtell's letter, why have the police more to do with Aborigines that anyone else? Could it be that the police are needed to quell disturbances caused by the Aborigines' consumption of cheap wine and metho peddled to them behind hotels by unscrupulous whites?

Mr Sawtell seems terrified of "drunken Aborigines", as I seem to remember this phrase also used in a previous letter of his. Drunkenness, be it in a black man or white, is not a pretty spectacle. I have seen a white man cut another's face with a broken bottle, and many other similar scenes. I cannot see why an aboriginal should be any more dangerous drunk than a white.

It is time that more say was given to members of the Aboriginal race (and there are many educationally qualified to have a say), and less to whites on the Aborigines' Welfare Board whose paternalistic attitude must be a constant insult to the more educated members of the race.

THE TRIAL OF GARY POWERS

On August 18th, 31-year-old American, Francis Gary Powers, pilot of a U-2 spy plane, pleaded guilty to espionage at his trial in Moscow. When the Court finished reading his long indictment, he said simply "Yes, I plead guilty."

A large press gallery was present, including 140 foreign correspondents representing 30 news agencies, and 90 newspapers, radio stations and television systems. None of these were aware in advance of his plea, and there had been expectation of a juicy trial and drawn-out controversy. So his admission of guilt came as a surprise.

But, from the American point of view, it was the only sensible thing to do. Powers had been flying 1,200 miles inside Russian territory. He had been shot down, and parachuted to safety, and captured, and his plane had crashed below, but in remarkably good condition. It was no use saying, as the Americans did early, that he was only a few miles inside Russia, or that it was a slight pilot error. He was clearly caught in the act, and Powers and the Americans wisely pleaded guilty.

His wife and parents were at the trial. The father had phoned President Khrushchev and asked for leniency. He had been received courteously, and it was explained to him that Mr K was in no position to interfere with the legal system, but he was sympathetic as a father and he would do whatever little he could.

On display in the Court, were photographic equipment and radio technical devices taken from the U-2, a tape recorder, parachute, pressurised flying suit, pistol, and a suicide poison pill for Powers if he chose to use it. Powers was recruited by the CIA specifically for such flights, and had been trained for 18 months. He told the Court that he was from a working-class family, and wanted to get money to start a business. He had never belonged to a political party, and had never voted.

He joined the Air Force because he could not get a good job after he left college, and he did not want to be called up for the infantry. He added that he was not asked if he wanted to take the mission; "I could not refuse. It was an order. I would have been considered a coward. And it would have meant the unsuccessful completion of my contract." He added that he had not been tortured in any way, and had been well treated since capture.

On the third day of the trial, Powers was allowed to address the Court before sentencing. He said "I confess that I have committed a very serious crime and merit punishment. I am a man who is deeply repentant and profoundly sorry for what he has done. I realise that the Russian people regard me as an enemy. But I do not feel, nor never have, enmity towards these people. I ask you to see me as a man who has never faced the court before on any charge, and who has realised his guilt."

The Prosecutor was of the opinion that "Powers is no robot. He is no ordinary spy, but a carefully trained criminal. He was no robot, who voluntarily sold himself for money. He deliberately committed a crime of such seriousness that it cannot be measured by the usual standards."

The three-Judge panel quickly made its sentencing decision. The maximum allowable for the crime was fifteen years. Powers was given 10 years. US President Eisenhower in Washington said that he regretted the severity of the sentence, but he must have been secretly quite relieved, in fact, that it had not been more.

The trial quickly faded from Western papers, but not so from Russian propaganda. On every possible occasion for 30 years, the mismanagement of this galling situation was brought up to haunt the Americans, and always it produced a reaction that showed how deeply the whole incident had hurt.

Powers was released in a prisoner-exchange programme after 21 months in captivity. He received a cold reception upon his return to the United States. Initially, he was criticized for having failed to activate his aircraft's self-destruct charge designed to destroy the camera and photograhic equipment, and also classified parts of his aircraft, before capture. In addition, others criticised him for deciding not to use an optional CIA-issued suicide-pills or cyanide capsule. However, a year later, he appeared before a Senate Armed Service Select Committee, and was declared "a fine young man who conducted himself well under dangerous circumstances."

He died, at age 41, in a helicopter crash when returning from fighting bushfires in California.

LETTERS FROM FOUR ANGRY MEN

Letters, D Hughes. I am considering sending the following letter to the Commissioner of Taxation. "In reply to your request to send a cheque, I wish to inform you that the present state of my account makes it impossible. My shattered financial position is due to provincial laws, town laws, liquor laws, sisters-in-laws, mothers-in-law and outlaws. Through these laws, I am compelled to pay income-tax, super-tax, sales-tax, tariff-tax, payroll-tax, and amusement-tax, also railway-tax.

"I am required to get a business licence, motor licence, marriage licence, radio licence, TV licence, telephone licence, and dog licence. I am asked to contribute to every society and organisation that man is capable of bringing to life, to unemployment relief and every hospital in the country.

"For my safety, I have to carry life insurance, third-party insurance, property insurance, liability insurance, fire insurance, earthquake insurance, war-risk insurance and unemployment insurance. I am suspected, inspected, disrespected, rejected, and ejected, examined and re-examined, informed and required, summonsed and fined, commanded and compelled until I supply an inexhaustible supply of money for every known need, desire and hope of the human race."

Letters, HOLDER. In accordance with the Police Commissioner's advice, I each year notify Chatswood police before going away on my holidays.

I have never yet had any acknowledgement of my letters. Apart from the fact that this does not inspire much confidence, it is surely bad public relations from the police point of view.

Letters, H Wilkinson, Woolloomooloo. I would like to know by what authority Mr G Dusseldorp, of Lend Lease Corporation, contends that the inner city is becoming the breeding ground for vice, and that the environment of big cities toady is not conducive to high ideals.

Does he contend that his destruction of Sydney's beautiful foreshores and the consequent loss of many homes in favour of concrete and glass monstrosities is to the ultimate advantage of Australians? Let us have replacement of slum dwellings at the hands of those whose activities are prompted primarily by consideration of family life, with due attention to the needs of our old folk and those of us who are not as affluent as Mr Dusseldorp.

It seems to me that the average Australian was far better off in pre-war days, when at least a mother could afford to stay at home and tend her family, when an ordinary bloke prepared to work could pay his way and afford to buy what is now to many of us in the luxury class – plenty of butter, a Sunday roast, and even a day out.

Letters, M Macleod. The statement by the NSW Minister for Labour and Industry, Mr Maloney, that the general principles of shopping hours were laid down in 1936 and the inference that nothing has happened to warrant a review is a dismaying example of archaic thinking. It is symptomatic of Labor's refusal to move with the times in an age of change.

In the past 24 years, tremendous changes have taken place both here and abroad, and this applies in no small measure to our shopping habits and requirements.

In many overseas countries, the shops are kept open for much longer hours than in NSW, and also on several nights a week, in order to provide the public with a first-rate service. The staff are not required to work more than 40 hours, and are on a roster system with adequate compensation for any additional hours worked.

What can be the Government's objection to introducing more sensible, and convenient shopping hours, particularly if both the stores and the staffs are agreeable. Wake up Mr Maloney: this is 1960, not 1936.

THE MAITLAND MURDERS

On the last day of August, Terrence Patrick O'Connor appeared before Mr Justice Brereton in the NSW Supreme Court on trial for the murder and decapitation of a couple at East Maitland.

Next day, after hearing all the evidence, the judge reconstructed the murders. He said that probably the killer, Mr O'Connor, came to the victim's house when the woman was in bed, and the husband was in night attire. The man, Sidney Shelley, may have heard a noise and gone to the door. The killer then shot at the door just as he opened it. He then went into the bedroom and shot Mrs Shelley while she was perhaps asleep. It appeared he silenced the 10-months-old baby by putting bed clothes over it.

O'Connor then dragged the body of the woman to the side of the bed and cut her head off with a 15-inch kitchen knife. Then he dragged Sidney's body over the front doorstep, where he cut off his head and put it in a bag.

The Judge said the reason for cutting off the head would have been to prevent recovery of bullets. These could have matched with bullets from the same pistol recovered from a clothesline post in the back yard, and thereby used to identify O'Connor's gun.

O'Connor, when asked if he had anything to say, said "Why should I kill a man I had only known for a few days, and a woman I had never met?" He was sentenced to life imprisonment.

DOGS IN SPACE

News item, August 21. Russia announced that two dogs were now tripping round space at 18,000miles per hour at a height of 180 miles above Earth. They were fired into space two days ago, along with other unidentified animals. The satellite that contains them is orbiting this nation five times a day, and in a few days time, would be visible in the twilight hours in the south east. More specific details would be available in a few days.

The spaceship, called SPUTNIK V, might be in orbit for as much as a month, though there is a possibility that it could be recalled in a few days. As usual, it was expected that the animals aboard would survive the re-entry, and would be rehabilitated successfully.

TRADING HOURS

Letters, R Mason. You reported that a men's barber was prosecuted for trading 15 minutes after the official closing time. Let us consider other occupations.

For a start, let us close the doors of hospitals at 5pm on the dot. Then there are ambulance stations and fire brigades to consider. Do any of the members quibble over extra time if an emergency arises at 4.55 or thereabouts?

Frankly, the opposition to petrol sales after hours is childish to say the least. This is the twentieth century and modern methods should be adopted. Why should the people be unable to purchase petrol if they need it at midnight? The same applies to other essential commodities. Doctors do not refuse a reasonable request for aid in the early hours of the morning.

This is supposed to be a democratic country, but lately I have had my doubts.

SEPTEMBER: MAX GLUCKMAN

At the start of the month, Paul Hasluck, the Minister for Territories, refused a visa for a visit to New Guinea by Professor Max Gluckman, from Manchester University. The scholar was the Head of the School of Social Anthropology at that University and had a long record of innovative and successful research into the causes and consequences of the systems of conflict that pertained in primitive societies, mainly in Africa. He was also, at the time, a visiting Fellow at the Australian National University. He was widely published, and had earned the deep respect of academics right round the world.

The Government refused to give a reason for his exclusion. Hasluck simply said it was on "advice received". This hoity-toity attitude drew the response from Labor's Jim Cairns. "Star Chamber answers like that have already gone too far in Australia. If the Professor is a security risk, what harm can he do in New Guinea in three weeks? I fail to see what damage he can do, unless there is a suspicion about his wife, who used to be a Communist. But she is not out here with him."

Civil libertarians and the University communities were outraged. They arose as one and attacked the Government. The letters below show some of their indignation. But the Government remained unmoved. It did not change its position, and it absolutely refused to explain itself. There were Governmental suggestions that he had been banned because of his sympathy towards Communist causes in Africa, but no one could take that seriously given the well-documented track record of Gluckman.

Letters, Mrs M Robertson. Let us assume the worst. Suppose the professor is a Communist. What does the Government think he would do in New Guinea?

If he committed an unlawful act while in New Guinea, or in Australia, he could be dealt with by the law. Customs authorities could search him to see that he didn't take in any bombs to throw about, nor steal any native secrets to sell to the Russians.

Of course he might criticise the Australian Administration but he wouldn't be the first and certainly won't be the last so long as gross inequalities such as very discriminatory wage rates exist in New Guinea.

Since when has the Australian Government assumed the right to punish a man before he does anything wrong? Or is it wrong to be a Communist, married to an ex-Communist, suspected of being a Communist, suspected of being sympathetic to Communism, or whatever category it is that the Security Service has placed the professor in?

Some years ago the Commonwealth Government sought to ban Communism but this aim was defeated at the ballot box. It isn't a crime to be a Communist, there is no law in the land that says that Communism is illegal.

The case of the professor is indeed serious. Under the pretext of anti-Communism, all critics or possible critics of the Government can be deprived of their rights. We enter into an "Alice in Wonderland" atmosphere where democracy is saved by the destruction of democracy.

The Federal Government has praised itself time and time again for its administration in New Guinea. Why then fear the visit for three weeks of one man, Communist or otherwise? If the Government has done as it says, then it has nothing to fear; or must we assume, as the Government has done with the Professor, that things are not as they appear on the surface?

Letters, R Spann, Professor of Government, University of Sydney. It so happens that I was a colleague of Gluckman for over four years at the University of Manchester, and during that time we became close friends. I attended many of his seminars, was often at his house with students, and belonged with him to many local societies. So I feel that I am in a special position to testify to his integrity. He had strong views on a variety of topics, but his only fanatical interest was in anthropology.

If he can be shown to be a security risk, I will publicly consume a copy of the Saturday edition of your estimable newspaper.

Letters, W Geddes, Professor of Social Antrhopology, University of Sydney. In Red China completely, and in the Soviet Union to a large extent, genuine social anthropology has ceased to exist. My last important contact in China, Dr Fei Hsiao-tung, recently was sent to a labour camp in Manchuria. Thus social anthropology is likely to incur distrust from both sides of the fence. The basic reason for this distrust is not the political creed of the anthropologists, but their necessary refusal to conform automatically to the ruling creed of their society. They must observe objectively and interpret honestly according to whatever theories they believe most valid, and their worth as scientists can be judged by the degree of their objectivity and honesty.

In this regard Professor Gluckman stands most high. He is as honest and open in his general views as any man in the Australian Parliament. He has as a citizen spoken at times against current Government policies, but he has also usually been right, and it is due to the criticisms of persons like him that British policy in Africa has been saved from some of the worst mistakes of other colonial Powers.

Even before this case arose, it was becoming clear that a protest must be made against the permit policy of the Department of Territories. **Several anthropologists have been refused entry.** Other appointees to university staffs have been warned in advance that they will be refused if they apply, and the universities have had to consider the consequences of appointing them under these conditions.

Also the knowledge of the possibility of permit refusal on future occasions definitely restricts the expression of views by anthropologists who do succeed in getting into the Territory. Politicians are great critics themselves. Why should they want to suppress the criticism of others, denying them the right they exercise and enjoy freely?

Communism is not involved in Professor Gluckman's case, but permits for other persons have been refused on grounds of Communist affiliation. This may be a valid reason if the person is currently or has recently been a party member. But in the cases which have come to my knowledge, the connection is long past and was very temporary. It is not strange that young persons developing an interest in social problems should at one stage have flirted with Communism, especially in earlier years before the issues became clear. I consider that in these cases too the attitude of the Department of Territories is wrong.

It must be realised that the Government freely admits to the Territory many persons with whose views about native peoples it is presumably not in accord, including certain sects of missionaries and certain kinds of businessmen. But it may exclude people whose conscience and commonsense make them public protagonists of native rights.

The Australian Government is not, as certain English papers have suggested, alone to blame in this case. Equally responsible are the British authorities which send ridiculous secret security reports to Australia. But Australia, after all, is an independent country, and need not act blindly on these reports, which the British Government itself would interpret differently.

Letters, J Woolcott, Mosman. Surely if Mr Khrushchev is able to visit America, Mr Gluckman may visit New Guinea!

Letters, L Durrant, Balgowlah. The Gluckman-is-undesirable-but-we-won't-say-why action is, to anyone who values the principles on which our society is founded, both detestable and frightening. This is gross misuse of governmental power – murder most foul of a man's reputation and arbitrary limitation of his freedom – carried out in totalitarian style by those who have been elected to act on behalf of the people of Australia.

All the gold medals of Rome will not sweeten the stink of this country's name in the world until this shockingly unliberal decision is reversed, with due apology, or fully explained and justified.

Comment. This whole incident raised apprehensions in some people about the Government's intentions concerning national security. At this time, it was amending the dreaded Crimes Act. This Federal Act had long been used for matters such as treason and sabotage to give the Government powers to by-pass normal protections afforded by British and Australian laws and, it was often said, introduce a police state. This was, in practice, an exaggeration, but any extension of the Crimes Act in this nation is always accompanied by a feeling of deep concern among those people worried about the preservation of our nation's liberties.

Then there was the question of whether the ban was imposed just to stir up fear in the community that the Communists were becoming active in New Guinea. Granted, the

Government had misjudged the situation badly, and it had misfired on them. But, the easiest way in the past to get extensions to the Crimes Act, or to win elections, had been simply to breed paranoia with more Reds-Under-the-Beds talk. Perhaps the wily and astute Menzies had tried this on this occasion.

Finally, the incident raised the whole issue of where the balance lies between national security on the one hand, and the rights of citizens on the other. This has long been a perplexing issue, and it remains one today (in 2020). For example, should captors have the right to torture prisoners to get so-called security information from them? Granted, this right has been much abused in the past, but on the other hand it had provided much information that had been legitimately useful for security. In this case, could the Government simply say "no" to Gluckman, and not explain why? And hide behind security secrecy? Perplexing as the question was then, and still is now, it turned out that the government **could** do just that, and in fact, **it did.**

A REPORT ON GRAHME THORN

NSW Police announced today that they had several useful new leads in the hunt for Graeme Thorne's killer. They are looking for a man about five feet eight inches tall, of stocky build, olive complexion, and jet-black hair that protruded from beneath a cap. The car is a 1955 Customline sedan, iridescent blue in colour with a distinctive silver chrome strip along each side.

They indicated that the search is continuing.

A WORD OF CAUTION.

For the nation, things seemed pretty good at this stage. People were all working, buying and spending, having their barbies on Sundays, grizzling about the Government and the local Council, and generally having a good time. But there were a few worrying signs on the horizon. For example, the stock market had been booming for a year. No one ever believes this at the time, but this cannot go on forever. **Then this month there was a series of national trade figures that suggested that there might be trouble ahead.**

It could be that things might get a bit tougher over the next year.

BENEFITS FOR EX-SERVICEMEN

Below is a lament bemoaning the parsimonious and capricious nature of various compensatory schemes for ex-servicemen from WWI.

Letters, Jerry Fox,. Mr G Bryant (Labor, Vic.) is to be commended for his notion in the House of Representatives seeking increased medical benefits for ex-Servicemen of World War I

The Government's unfailingly parsimonious and frequently inconsistent attitude on this subject is a sore point with returned men who, it should be remembered, were all volunteers, and, practically without exception, became combat soldiers in combat units.

The Minister for Health, Dr A Cameron, appears to have made it clear that the onus of proof of disability arising from war service is on the

Serviceman himself. In this event, the Government holds all the trump cards.

When the origin of so many complaints is still not known under normal civilian conditions, how can it be said with certainty that a disease has arisen – or not arisen – through wartime service?

The right and proper course would be to provide free medical and hospital treatment for all those who served in combat units – and proof of such service should be the only requirement needed in order to qualify for these medical benefits.

Comment. Our returned men, of whatever war, never seem to get the compensation they deserve. Whether it is from the physical injuries of WWII, the exposure to atomic radiation at Woomera, the psychological damage of Vietnam, or the traumas of the Melbourne and Voyager disasters, there is always much fumbling and obstructionism and delay for decades until the number of claimants has been reduced by deaths.

OUTPATIENTS AT HOSPITALS

Letters, Out-Patient, King's Cross. Some days ago I had occasion to go to one of Sydney's large hospitals, and found the arrangements for out-patients deplorable.

I sat in a very cold and draughty corridor, where, incidentally, I caught a severe chill and was laid up for a week. The doctor was 20 minutes late. After examining me, he ordered an X-ray. This was carried out expeditiously. On returning for the report on the X-ray the doctor, who was 65 minutes late, told me to make an appointment with the orthopaedic surgeon.

I was herded into a small waiting-room with insufficient chairs and I discovered from one of the nurses that everyone had been given an appointment for 1.30. There were 20 patients and numerous others undergoing treatment. At 2.30, an hour later, not one patient had been called, which meant that the last patient would have been waiting four and a half hours at the least. By now thoroughly disgusted, I forfeited all I had paid and made an appointment with a Macquarie Street specialist.

The fact that everyone had been given an appointment for the same time shows either a want of organisation or indifference to what happens to patients.

Comment. I think everyone across the nation who has had recent contact with our emergency and casualty outpatient systems can report long waiting times, sometimes inadequate service, and even negligence and mistakes in procedures and treatments that have cost lives. It is hard to see much change there over the years, and sadly I gauge the cause to be still the same as it was fifty year ago, in that the various workers in that system are still overworked and generally dog-tired.

AUTOMATIC VENDING MACHINES

By 1960, several other States had been using the vending machines successfully for over two years. But in NSW, the opponents were adamant. They argued that spillage of petrol was a danger, that huge explosions were imminent, and that ordinary citizens would suffer inhalation problems. Of course, the true reason was that it was obvious that driveway attendants would lose their jobs, and so the Unions were now seriously dragging their feet. They managed to stall for another couple of years, and then the thrust of public pressure forced change on them.

Comment. With all the changes caused by technology over the last fifty years, everyone has reacted the same. It might be the drivers of those splendid lifts in the city stores, or the conductors on buses, or the young women who manned the telephone exchanges. In the face of a compelling new technology, they put off the evil day for as long as possible, and talked about anything except the real issue, which was the loss of jobs and revenue and profits. Despite the fact that some things change, some things never change.

FOUR WEEKS ANNUAL LEAVE

The Sydney County Council, at the end of September, **granted 4-weeks annual leave to all of its employees**. It was about the first NSW body to do this, and there were fears that the new provision would spread from that Council to all other Councils, and from there to the entire workforce. "The economy can't afford it" was the concerted cry from employers.

Comment. Over the years, virtually all employers now **do** afford it. And they afford long service leave, and maternity leave, and compassionate leave. They also provide for part-time work, and air-conditioning in offices and many factories, and safety regulations that are at least part-way effective.

DELAYS IN CONVEYANCING

Letters, SOLICITORS. Does the general public realise that solicitors, conveyancers, legal search clerks and private people often have to wait day by day, week by week and, in one case in our office, month by month) before they can complete the search of the title of any piece of land?

When the searchers put their requirements on the counter, they have to wait as long as one hour and a half before they are picked up and dealt with. Then, as often as not, the answer is, "The book is out" "The book is lost!" "We don't know where the book is!"

It is estimated that these highly paid search clerks are paid at the very minimum four times as much for the period they stand in a queue as for the period they are actually searching. In addition to this, it is very often impossible to make final searches before settlement, and solicitors have to take the enormous risks that the title will not be in order when the transfer or mortgage is lodged for registration.

On one occasion our clerk informed us that additional office staff had been provided at the Registrar-General's Department and that one day her searching was easy. The next day things were just as bad as ever. She heard one private searcher complaining that he had waited for half an hour. An officer behind the counter replied almost jubilantly. "Only half an hour! Why, most people wait at least an hour and a half!"

We cannot believe that it is impossible to rectify the position, and we understand from our clerks that a considerable improvement has been made in the basement department, so that it should not be impossible to make the same improvement in other departments.

Comment. Right now, in 2020, you can get a Title search in a few minutes and at virtually no cost. The system in 1960, as was correctly described by SOLICITOR, was sheer agony.

THOUGHTS ON TEA TOWELS

Letters, Helena Winter. I read recently that doctors are perturbed at the illnesses some mothers contract while in hospital having their babies. Having been employed as a pantry maid at a maternity ward of Sydney's largest hospitals, may I suggest that the common tea towel be scrapped and the dishes coming from the maternity ward be scraped, rinsed in hot running water, washed in hot soapy water, rinsed again in hot running water and put on racks to dry. The alternative: use paper cups and plates.

Letters, P Hayley. Washing-up without using tea towels is the method we have used in my house for years with most satisfactory results. Knives, forks and spoons are rinsed with hot water from the sink heater while each other articles when taken out of the hot soapy dishwater are immediately held under the cold water tap before being put in the drainer.

Washing of tea towels is thus avoided, and everything dries quickly with a shiny surface. There is less trouble than with the ancient method.

Letters, Mary Kinnell, Terrigal. I agree with Helena Winter, except for one thing. For the first rinse of dirty dishes, cold water is best. If they have either starches or proteins clinging to them, hot water only makes the food stick harder. But for greasy dishes, the first rinse should be hot. Then wash all the dishes in hot soapy water, rinse again in hot running water, and then place them on a rack to dry.

ENVIROMENTAL MATTERS

Letters, NOISE HATER. Is there a society for the abatement of noise in Sydney? If there is, I would most urgently importune it to use its influence to force the Transport Department to withdraw the accursed whistles it issues to its conductors.

I cannot see any earthly reason why the department persists in this practice, as there is on every type of bus ample provision in the way of bells and bell-cords to let the driver know when it is safe to start the bus.

And there is nothing more excruciating than to hear this shrill whistle, particularly when one is absorbed in thought or immersed in his daily newspaper.

Letters, A Garner, Kingswood, Victoria. Travelling from Sydney by train, I was delighted by the beautiful green aspect of the country as far as one could see, and giving promise of a most bountiful season. This was on the Albury line, and the greenery was equal to a well-developed suburban lawn.

However, one could not help being struck with the very great extent of soil erosion. Assuming the same applies to the country beyond view from the train, the loss of soil must amount to thousands of acres.

I understand that where great earthmoving projects are taking place elsewhere, the bared soil and slopes must have suitable grass seeds combined with an adhesive forced into the soil. As the seed germinates, the adhesive dissolves, acting as a fertiliser.

Surely similar action could be taken with this soil erosion. If the equipment required is too expensive for individual landowners, co-operation is the answer. Thousands spent now means millions in the future.

Letters, G Gutz, Armidale. I get fed up with your Letter writers. On any day, over half the space is taken up with self-important spokesmen, and politicians, and government sycophants writing Letters that are too long, full of selective statistics, and pushing some policy or other. Why can't they say that we want something to happen, because we will get money or jobs out of it?

Then there are goody-goody writers like yesterday's Mr Garner from Victoria. They take a couple of looks out of a train window and decide they can fix the erosion problem. They have no inkling that this has been a major problem for years, and that measures on a grand scale are being done to meet the problem. But no, the writer decides that he knows the answer, and has the immediate solution that thousands of others have overlooked.

Give me simple one-thought Letters, with simple reasons, and cut the cackle.

REMEMBER PEN-FRIENDS?

Right across the world, writers were keeping in touch with other writers as pen-friends. A lot of these were found by placing adds like this in newspapers and magazines.

Letters, Jacqueline Einstein, South Africa. I am a South African girl, aged 14. My family intends to settle in Sydney at the end of the year. I would like to correspond with a few Australian boys and girls to get an idea of life in your country.

I hope you will help me by publishing this letter.

Comment. Today, I suspect, this exciting practice has died out with the advent of Facebook and Twitter. That is a pity in the sense that the arrival and consideration of a letter from a far-flung location always created a thrill.

A 280-word letterette via Twitter, shared with the world, does not do that.

OCTOBER: THE GREATEST SHOW ON EARTH

By the start of April, the greatest collection of political leaders the world had ever seen had gathered in New York. It would have been nice to think they had gathered there seeking peace and harmony, under the auspices of the United Nations. Perhaps they might stop the arms race, and perhaps they might reduce the huge stockpile of atom and hydrogen bombs. Perhaps they might stop their stupid point-scoring and bickering, and work on creating friendships that would give peace and economic prosperity to all. But, **No! That was not possible. This was the Cold War.**

The great influx into New York was started by our old Russian friend, Nikita Khrushchev. You remember he had walked away from scheduled talks in Paris, and left the Western leaders with no one to score points off. Now, he decided that he wanted some free publicity in the Western Press, and that the next meeting of the UN was the place to get it. So he announced his intention to attend. But, as cagey as ever, he organised that the leaders of most of the Communist bloc countries would also attend. So a dozen Red despots arrived in New York at the end of September, ready to do battle with the capitalist pigs from the Western World.

A year ago, when Mr K was last in America, he had been quite politely received. The Press had been instructed to be polite, and print nothing antagonistic. But this time, it was very different. After all, Mr K had rubbished the Paris talks, and then Russia had tried the spy, Powers. So, he was distinctly a persona not at all grata. He was met at the dock by protestors jeering and catcalling, and carrying banners reading "gravedigger of the world - scram" and "killer of Russian people". He was also called a murderer, gangster, hangman, exterminator, monster and liar.

Fidel Castro of Cuba was also on the guest list. He had not yet gone over fully to the Communist side, though he was clearly a bit shaky. So he was given a hysterical welcome by hundreds of adoring women, many of them in white bobby-sox. It was reported that the Castro fans were encouraged by women cheerleaders who waved revolutionary white and blue flags. At one stage, an American blond broke from the crowd and stretched her arms towards his window. "I don't care what his politics are. He's a real hunk of a man."

At about the same time, national leaders from the Western world had decided that they too should spend a week at the UN, so the top men from countries like Britain and France and drifted into New York with as much fanfare as they could muster. Our own "world's best orator" Prime Minister, Bob Menzies, after watching the circus for a week, decided to join it, so he too packed his bags. He, of course, along with the other leaders from the Western alliance, missed out on all the fun that Khruschchev and Castro were getting, and were received instead with all the pomp and ceremony befitting such worthy dignitaries.

In all, 98 States were present, and there were 21 heads of Governments. The New York Times said "The gathering can only be compared with the Congress of Vienna of 1814, and the Versailles Conference of 1919. Never before have so many leaders gathered together to say so much to each other."

The UN speeches followed exactly the party lines adopted over the last few years. Castro was an early star. His speech was vigorous, though only in one aspect was it remarkable. He attacked the US for its colonialism and aggression, he said that the US had exploited Cuba for years before his Revolution, and that Vice-President Nixon and Senator Kennedy were ignorant. He added, robustly, that his delegation had been given dreadful accommodation in New York, and that the women had been housed in a brothel. The only remarkable part was that **it took four-and-a-half hours**, so that he ended up so completely hoarse that he was compelled to stop. **But, he kept his shoes on.**

A few days later, Harold McMillan, the British Prime Minister, took to the lectern ready to pontificate. This thoroughly British gentleman was famous for his speeches in the House of Commons, where he mouthed the most platitudinous statements that could be imagined, and made them sound quite wondrous. He spoke about the plans of the West for disarmament, and once again re-assured the world that the British way was the only way. But he strayed on to the subject of Mr K's not attending the Paris talks. At this point, Khrushchev jumped to his feet, started to wave his arms around, thump tables, and interjected ceaselessly in Russian. He was in an obvious rage, and calls for "order" from the Chair did nothing to subdue him. It was a scene never before witnessed in the UN, and it lasted for ten minutes. Delegates were astounded, and doubtless well satisfied that they had not wasted their money in coming. After the Session was over, the two leaders had a private kiss-and-make-up meeting for two hours, but at the end would only say that their positions were unchanged.

Mr McMillan held his cool throughout, and the major points were heard by all, so that despite the uproar, he could glow in the report that "Non-Communist diplomats praised the substance, style and delivery of his speech, and described it as one of the most brilliant in UN history." Other were not so impressed. Dr Koto Matsuaira, the Japanese representative, merely said "It was very good, very complete." But, in any case, **he kept his shoes on**.

But, by now, Mr K was getting warmed up. So a week later he went back to the UN and spoke again. I will leave it to Associated Press (mainly) to describe the event. "He lumbered onto the dais and started to storm. He took the position that the West was trying to frighten him. "We won't be bullied. We won't be scared. If you want to compete with us in the arms race, we will beat you at that. Our rockets will come out like sausages from the machine. Do you want to try us out?'

He went on. "We are not to be scared at red cloths. We are Communists. Our nerves are strong. Do you scare us with such arguments? You haven't got the guts to do it. We are not afraid of war. If a war is foisted on us, we will be victorious regardless of sacrifices. But the losses will be uncountable and appalling. Some of you will not be here if a nuclear war breaks out."

A United Press correspondent said "Khrushchev was white-faced, shouting. The veins on his forehead stood out as he spilled out intemperate, often vulgar words. He even ridiculed Americans for chewing gum. He compared the Paris talks, broken off in June, to a stable, and the stench therein. "Let's spit on that institution and get out." He was by turns irate, bitter, vulgar and vituperative. The West was, of course shocked by this. The Communist block was, of course, delighted, and applauded wildly. The diplomats from the Non-aligned nations were, of course, diplomatic. But throughout it all, **he did not take off any shoes**.

That brings me to the punchline of the shaggy–dog story I have been telling. As you have all guessed by now, I have been leading up to someone or other who **did** take off a shoe or two. And it would not be hard to work out who that person would be. Well, then, you were all right – it was our friend Mr K, and he did it in the UN on the last day of proceedings before everyone went home. He started off by interrupting other speakers while they spoke. He described, by shouting, the Philipine delegate as a "servile, fawning creature, happy in subservience", then took off his shoe and made a motion as if to throw it at the President of the Assembly. He kept on shouting and banging his desk with the shoe, and gradually made his way to the dais. Once there, he continued to brandish his shoe, shouting slogans mingled with abuse, while the President broke his gavel calling for order. But it was too late. The entire place was in uproar, with many delegates now clustered round the rostrum, but there was no point because the electricity had been cut off. The President gave up, and declared the Session closed. Some delegates then stopped their arguing long enough to cheer, others chose instead to boo, but either way, this "most remarkable Session of the UN ever seen" had come to a close.

Comment. It was a great circus. No serious thoughts about disarmament were discussed, and everyone came away fully entrenched in their previous positions. The same was true of Khrushchev. He was seen as either a bigger hero, or a bigger villain, depending on what you thought at the beginning. But the already-dubious standing of the UN was damaged, as millions and millions of people throughout the world shrugged it off for the future.

Postscript. Our own Mr Menzies made a speech that was widely criticised, especially by the Non-Aligned nations. The *Sydney Herald* took a cudgel to him for that, and a correspondent came back and supported him with a Letter. **The Herald closed the matter with a Comment.**

I have published that final Letter, and the Comment. Not because of the content of either, because such minor disagreements were commonplace. Rather, it is because of the bewilderment I felt as I read **the Comment.** Of course, people more erudite than I am will be familiar with the reference and its meaning, but I put it here because I think most readers will enjoy sharing with me their own bewilderment.

Letters, Mary Evans, Woollahra. The tendency for the Herald to gibe at Mr Menzies on every possible occasion becomes quite tedious. A refusal on his part to attend the present meeting of the UN at the request of the Prime Minister of Great Britain would have been very insulting indeed especially in view of the critical position of world affairs. It must indeed be galling to the Herald to feel that the PM of Australia is held in high esteem as a statesman beyond the confines of his own country.

Editor's Comment. Let the galled jade wince, our withers are unwrung.

STEPEN LESLIE BRADLEY

On October 10, Stephen Leslie Bradley, a poker-machine mechanic from the Sydney seaside suburb of Manly, was arrested on board a liner when it berthed in Colombo. He will be charged with the kidnapping and murder of the boy.

Bradley was arrested by local police, though two Australian detectives were then on their way by plane. Police in Australia had recently seized a blue sedan car owned by Bradley, and impounded a Pekinese dog, owned by him, from a kennel at King's Cross. They had earlier found Pekinese hairs on the rug that wrapped round Graeme's body. They had also taken samples of soil from a Bradley-connected house on the North Shore. It was reported that "painstaking checking and close collaboration with the CIB Scientific Bureau enabled the police to issue the warrant for the arrest with confidence."

It was believed that Bradley would be readily extradited, even though no formal Treaty with Colombo existed. Bradley's wife and three children will continue on board the Himalaya to Versailles.

Over the next few weeks, Bradley was formally charged and a local Counsel took up his defence, free of charge. After some legal scuffles in the court, Bradley was committed for trial in NSW, and his extradition was organised for the end of the month.

Comment. It was great to see justice being done. But the fact of the tragedy remained for his family and friends. It was also the beginning of a new attitude in Australia. We had always considered ourselves as being immune to such "American" crimes as kidnapping. Now we found we were not. As the years went on, and more cases emerged, like the Beaumonts much later, it became too obvious to us that real threats existed, and we started to impose ever-increasing security on our children. As someone put it, the Thorne case was the call for us as a nation to wake up from our "age of innocence."

THE RABBIT MENACE

Letters, H Wood. The CSIRO has called a conference of those interested in a war that has gone on for nearly a century with the rabbit still unconquered.

Whereas the merino has been consciously and carefully bred, not so the rabbit, except that maybe the methods aimed at his extermination have eliminated the unfit, and developed a type adaptable to his environment.

Imagine what the rabbit might be if he received the same scientific attention as the sheep. Considering the world shortage of food, it is heinous to exterminate the rabbit instead of controlling and developing him from a pest to an asset. The flesh is delectable, and the fur as valuable as wool. Considering his size, he surpasses sheep and cattle in edible and fabric categories.

All our domestic animals and poultry, and our fruit, vegetables and cereals (many of them pests in ages gone) have been developed from their wild ancestors by careful, thoughtful cultivation. In some countries, fur farming is successfully practised; why not with the rabbit in Australia?

Instead of concentrating on the production of futile rabbit poisons, let the CSIRO try to deal with the problem in a constructive manner by working out a practical plan to make the rabbit a national asset beneficial to the Australian community, its farmers and graziers, and the world in general.

Letters, G Chislett, Sec., Aust. Woolgrowers' Council, Sydney. Mr H Spencer-Wood must be fishing for a bite when he proposes the conservation of the rabbit rather than its destruction. However, this is a matter on which we cannot afford to be facetious, or to make rash claims about "delectable" flesh and "valuable" fur, nor to romanticise about solving the food shortage.

The loss to the nation caused by the introduction of the rabbit in terms of money and natural assets would run to hundreds of millions of pounds if it were possible to assess it accurately. Reckoning on the basis of about eight rabbits displacing one sheep, it is dismaying to contemplate how much foreign exchange earnings has been forgone in the past because of the depredations of the rabbit, which, at the same time, has caused vast destruction to our pastures.

Whether the flesh is delectable and the fur valuable is a matter of opinion in the first case and the market in the other, but we need not waste our energy on these considerations since, related to sheep meats and wool values, they are beaten on both scores.

As for combating the world food shortage with rabbit meat, the so-called food "shortage" is an economic problem rather than a production problem. The primary producers of the world are more than capable of feeding everyone, if only some way could be perfected for getting available surplus food, including meats, to the needy.

Complacency about the rabbit scourge could cost us dearly if we default on the opportunity for eradicating this pest, presented to us through the effects of myxomatosis.

Letters, Bill Williams. I wish to support Spencer-Wood's view of the rabbit as a possible national asset. Rabbit-farming should be legalised; present prices of rabbit carcasses and skins make them a valuable asset. This could begin an industry like poultry-farming.

The sheep farmer wire-nets his fences to keep the rabbits out, so if you can fence them out you can fence them in. Rabbit farms could be registered to see they are rabbit-retaining.

The rabbit farmer could ferret them out on either enclosed or Crown lands, thus putting the rabbit under control.

NOVEMBER: TOUGH TIMES NOW CLOSER?

November started, as it often does, with the first day of the month. But this first day was somewhat special, because it was also the first Tuesday. In fact it was the first Tuesday in November. In Australia. And that, of course, meant Melbourne Cup Day.

So, that day, the newspapers were all light and airy. There were hundreds of reports on the Cup, and there could be no doubt that Tulloch, a real champion, would win despite the huge weight he would carry.

Then for Sydney, there was added excitement, because today the Cup **would be telecast live** there for the first time. For those who preferred more solemn matters, there was the ever-hopeful news that the Archbishop of Canterbury was about to formally visit the Pope. Maybe various moves for Christian unity would thus be furthered. John Wayne, the American film star, was expecting a child. Even the Shah of Persia made the front pages that day with the birth of a long-awaited son and heir. Whacko! What a Beauty!!

(Here comes the inevitable "But".) But there were small clouds developing. Mr Menzies, and friends like Billy McMahon, had earlier in the year opened up our markets to allow more imports into the nation. Now, our foreign reserves were running down at a fast pace, and so the Government had just imposed rather severe restraints on the economy. They had raised Sales Taxes on all sorts of imported goods, including a "luxury" tax of 40 per cent on cars. Bank credit was hugely reduced to businesses, and home buyers were told "no way."

So there were a few dents appearing our prosperity. Then there was something of an epidemic of hepatitis. NSW was reporting about 40 cases a day, and that was worrying. There were also the problems of men and women with big bodies or feet, or small bodies or feet. They just could not find clothes and shoes to buy. The newspapers were full of letters and comments from groups like "The Tall Women's Society" complaining about this, and even threatening boycotts of the sellers who were not providing the goods they were now threatening not to buy.

Finally, here, everyone was concerned that the nation's Hire Purchase debt was growing too fast, with the prospect of large debts if the economy did enter a recession. This was clearly a big problem, but not big enough to stop the buying on the Never-Never. People wanted it now, and they got it now.

But on Melbourne Cup Day, none of these clouds mattered. Buy a ticket in the sweep, suddenly become an expert and tell everyone who the winner would be, have a bet with an SP bookie, sink a few beers per hour till dark, drive home half tanked, go to sleep in front of tellie. What a great day. Pity, though, you hadn't backed Hi Jinx. That would have been perfection.

THE OTHER SIDE OF THE WORLD

Britain is uneasy about the establishment of a US base for Polaris nuclear submarines at Holy Lock, 30 miles from Glasgow. Having already agreed to the creation of the base, the British government is locked in, but is now asking for guarantees from the US government that the missiles will not be fired unless the British first agree. The Americans will not give that guarantee.

They argue that the base would not be a target in times of conflict. They say that it will be used only for refurbishment, and only three subs will be there at any one time. Their British counterparts argue that the base is a sitting duck, and that it will be a prime target because if it were destroyed, the other subs would have no place to refurbish.

Further, they argue, the range of the missiles is 2,500 miles, and it is hard to believe that during conflict the subs would sit in port and not fire off their missiles. 95,000 Trade Unionists are meeting now to express "alarm" over this situation.

Comment. How lucky we were to be over here, so far from all these worries that plagued people from Britain to Russia.

THE US PRESIDENTIAL ELECTIONS

America, meanwhile, was just entering the final week of its election campaign. The candidates were John Kennedy, a Democrat, and Richard Nixon representing the Republicans. Both sides were vigorous in saying that on the one hand they were certain to win, and on the other that their supporters should not get too complacent lest they did not vote. But preliminary polls suggested that voting would be about equal, so activity in this week was hectic.

Richard Nixon scrubbed up well, and oozed confidence. But it was the youthful Kennedy who won the poll, 52% to 48%. The Democrats also won in both Houses, though it was not yet clear if they would have control of the Senate.

OUR CENSORS ON THE BALL

In early November, the British Censorship Board decided that the novel, Lady Chatterley's Lover, would be removed from a censorship ban that had been in place since 1928. The novel had been written by famous author D H Lawrence, and dealt with an affair between the aristocratic and attractive Lady Chatterley, and a younger gardener who became her lover. The Board had rejected the book on the basis of the foul language and because of some explicit sexual themes.

In 1960, Penguin books, realising that times had changed, deliberately sold the book openly, and thereby challenged the earlier findings of the Board. The decision was that the book could now be published and released in its original form. The various rulings in Australia were much slower to come, and indeed the Australia Post stilled banned the posting of the book in 2007.

Lawrence had died in 1932, and our interest in him is because the release of this book was an important symbolic step in the growth of women's rights in the 1960's, which will be covered in later books. But also he had been in Australia for a short time prior to his death, and that now generated some Letters of interest.

Letters, Bill English. If the ban on Chatterley is lifted here as in Britain, what a rush will take place to obtain the book. Bookshops will have the sell-out of their lives.

I wonder how many of the sensation-seekers will know or care that Lawrence lived for a time in our South Coast town, Coalcliff, and was a school teacher there, and wrote the novel "Kangaroo", which is of more literary value to this nation than any other he created.

Is it not time we preserve for future generations the houses where great pioneers of thought, as well as agriculture, have lived, if it is not too late? Has anything been done in Burwood to mark the house where Havelock Ellis lived?

Letters, W Bayley, Royal Australian Historical Society, Thirrool.   Lawrence did not live at Coalcliff but stayed for a few short weeks at nearby Thirrool in a house by the sea that still exists. In fact, his stay in Australia was brief. He was not a schoolteacher here.

His book, "Kangaroo" was written during the few weeks of his holiday at Thirrool and cannot highlight Australia as he was not in the country long enough to know much about it

The book is claimed to describe the South Coast but it is full of factual and geographical inaccuracies no doubt permissible to fiction writers. Lawrence travelled by train from Sydney to Mullumbimby by taking a train over Como Bridge and down to the South Coast. His description of the trip is wearying (perhaps because the trip by train was and still is, with all those gumtrees). The contribution of Lawrence to the progress of Thirrool was nil.

Letters, Charles Higham.   I was astonished by Mr Bayley's Letter. It is true that Lawrence's visit was brief, and that he fumbled some details of the local topography, but it is also true he described bush and coast with a poetic intensity not equalled by any Australian. To describe Lawrence's passages on the train ride through Como as "wearying" shows a lack of response to one of the most exquisite passages in the novel.

Letters, Catherine Mackerras.   When D H Lawrence's "Kangaroo" was first published in 1923, I reviewed it for "The Pacific", a now defunct Sydney fortnightly. Here is what I said:

"Many of us may dislike Mr Lawrence as an author; few will deny to him the gift of an exquisite prose style. He possesses an unsurpassed faculty for conveying impressions; and his descriptions of scenes and places are not merely descriptions; they are word-pictures in the most complete sense. More, they reach, in some mysterious fashion, the heart and soul of what they describe.

"Australians miss the subtle atmosphere of Australia when they are long absent from it, and when they return they respond to it, though they cannot define wherein it consists. But Mr Lawrence, the stranger, has defined it; he has caught and imprisoned in words the elusive charm of Sydney, the green beauty of the South Coast. The marvellous southern dawn 'more virgin than humanity can conceive', the nights 'raving with moonlight,' the Australian spring, 'with the perfume in all the air that might be Heaven' – never have these been so described.

"It is almost uncanny, as though the soul of Australia had indeed been captured by a magician, and crushed between the pages of a book." The passage of 37 years has not caused me to alter my final estimate of "Kangaroo".

"Altogether a strange, neurotic book, very characteristic of its author; but a book, however morbid, that no educated Australian can afford to leave unread, for its wonderful evocation of the Australian scene."

CURES FOR AILMENTS

Letters, G Drury, The Hague, Holland. I have been holidaying for a year in Holland, and recently heard of a cure for those unfortunate sufferers from rheumatism. One man I met, for years had been almost crippled with this complaint, but now seems completely restored to his former good health. His cure is a very simple one – he carries two chestnuts in his pocket.

Similarly, I can vouch that a nutmeg will effect much relief for the unfortunate sufferers from gout. I suffered periodic attacks of this distressing condition until I heard of the nutmeg cure while holidaying in New Zealand just over five years ago. I have never gone without the "cure" since then, and I can honestly say I have never suffered from an attack of gout.

Letters, Dorothea Sharland. Sufferers from cramp may be interested to know of a simple cure for rheumatism and gout. It is to carry a piece of camphor in the hip pocket or, for women, attached to the corset. I read of it in New Zealand and have proved it to be of decided value.

Letters, Hank Yeo. My old Mum before she passed on, used to recommend this cure for cramp. Spread treacle real thick on brown paper and apply.

Letters, Hugh Frewen. A higher grade of milk containing 5 per cent butter fat should be marketed. We should be prepared to consider the widespread public grievance in regard to the quality of Sydney's milk supply.

The cream content of milk is the appetiser that induces the milk-loving public to buy freely. If offered for sale, even at present prices, the increased demand and consumption would astound everybody. A lower-priced product with a 3.5 per cent far content could be supplied to meet "slimming" and "doctor's orders."

Advertisements and appeals to "drink more milk" are no substitute for quality.

My comment. This is a subject dear to my heart, and one that I never tire of complaining about. After the War, I could get milk delivered to my door by a milko with a horse and dray. It was drawn from 10 gallon drums, and carried to the jug on the front verandah in metal gaddens. Then it was left to settle, and form a beautiful head of cream. This was real milk.

By 1960, milk delivery was done with motorised vans, the milk itself mostly came in bottles, but now it was often homogenised. That means it had been stirred up and otherwise contorted so that the butterfat was spread evenly throughout, with no prospect of cream. Ghastly stuff.

Since then, as times and milk changed, the quality has gotten worse. Instead of milk at 5 per cent fat, then at 3.5 per cent, nowadays the stuff pushed on us "for health reasons" is 0.1 per cent, and called triumphantly "no-fat." Words fail me.

There is nothing I can easily do about this. For me, the milk terrorists have done their dastardly deed, and left the nation in ruins. All that is left for me is to hope – against hope – that future generations will somehow wake up to themselves, and that once again we will become the land of milk, real milk. Never mind the honey.

A NIB-LESS WORLD

When I was writing my 1948 book, I wrote "but now we were learning to write with pen and ink. We were using pens with nibs, and ink that came in ink-wells. Spills and blots were everywhere. Nibs were always clogging up with hair and paper fibres. They were always breaking. Every shirt had a six-inch immovable ink-stain across the pocket. Girls had their stains on their white bobby sox."

By 1960, the biro was making a strong bid to oust pen-and-ink, though the battle was not yet won.

Letters, J Sherwood. C Ramage suggests the pen-nib and ink are used by schoolchildren to produce the variation in thickness of the up and down strokes, which, he says, is necessary for good handwriting.

I consider it a matter of opinion whether or not a particular style of handwriting is "good". Also the variation in the thickness of the strokes was originally only due to a characteristic of the type of pens used in a bygone age.

To my mind, good handwriting is that which can be done easily and quickly, and which can also be read easily. I am sure the ballpoint pen can meet these requirements.

I agree that some styles of handwriting are more beautiful than others, but why not let it remain an art to be pursued by those who are interested? To most of us it is only a means to an end where legibility is the most important factor.

Letters, C Ramage. J Sherwood was wide of the mark when he deplored the use by schoolchildren of pen and ink instead of ballpoint pens.

The point is that the variation in thickness of up and down strokes so necessary to good handwriting cannot be obtained from ballpoint pens and, therefore, no interest is manifested in handwriting. In recent years there has been a really serious decline in the art.

Letters, J Sherwood. Many other departments would do well to follow the example set by the NSW Department of Railways and substitute ballpoint pens for the dirty and inefficient pen-nibs and ink of yesteryear.

In particular I am thinking of the Department of Education. I fail to see why children who are learning to write should struggle with scratchy pens and ink, which, in a child's hand, drips and smudges all over himself and his work. I believe the chief objection to the use of ballpoint pens in schools is that they destroy "character" in the child's handwriting. Maybe so, but I have not noticed any encouragement of individuality in the child' handwriting at school.

On the contrary, as far as I know, the children are expected to copy a standard form, in which case ballpoint pens would do no harm and would assist in achieving legibility, as there would be no ugly blots and smudges to obliterate the written work. Also there would be a lot less washing of ink-spattered clothes for mother to do, which is a serious consideration in the winter months when the heavier type of school uniform is worn.

WEST INDIES CRICKETERS ARE DUE

BE WARNED. At the end of November, these champions of the world's greatest sport had just about finished their preliminary games against the States, and were almost ready for the Tests against Australia's finest. Legendary figures such as Worrell, Hall, and Sobers were strutting the stages, and we had our own Benaud, O'Neil, and Harvey.

At about this time on every tour, the papers are full of Letters, all very excited about the prospects ahead, and some of them sensible and some of them not. See if you can work out which are which.

Letters, T Roughley. I was privileged to see that great innings of Cammie Smith on Saturday, and when it came to an untimely end my mind roamed back over the years to find a parallel for its daring, skill and grace. I surveyed all the great batsmen I have seen during the past 60 years, and found I had to go back to Victor Trumper to find such a parallel.

Never did Trumper "play himself in". From the moment he came to the crease his flashing bat pounded the ball to all points of the compass. The defence of his wicket seemed always to be a secondary consideration; every ball came to him as a challenge to hit it to the fence (or over it). And that was the outlook that seemed to inspire Cammie Smith on Saturday. He had much of Trumper's grace, and the power of his shots showed perfect timing.

I can't remember such disappointment when the innings of one of our opponents ended. It flashed with the brilliance of a meteor, and unfortunately ended just as suddenly.

Thank you, Cammie Smith. You've shown us once more that cricket can be a grand game, full of daring and excitement.

Letters, J Rhys Griffiths. Our visitors from the West Indies do not appear to understand the modern attitude to international cricket.

Seeing them last Saturday, one would think it was a game.

Letters, M McCauley. Mr C Kelly is reported in the "Herald" asking for the CSIRO to act quickly on cricket pitches. Surely cricket administrators already have done enough harm to the "Grand Old Game" by continually altering its rules.

The vagaries of cricket pitches supply the spice that makes cricket so interesting. The cricket associations should leave well alone or they can shut the gates. There is much more to cricket than making pitches a batsman's paradise.

MISS AUSTRALIA

In 1960, Rosemary Fention won this honour. After about this date, various womens' groups said that young ladies should be denied vying for this Title. By 1990, it looked as if the competition would fold. But sense prevailed. and it has drawn renewed strength, in a modified form, as the years progresed.

GAMBLING

Variious people, including clergy, were worried about gambling getting a grip on the population. The normal horse-racing was being supplemented by night trotting which was gaining popularity. Poker machines in clubs were still being developed, and these were designed to extract money from punters at a rapid rate.

Then there was planty of talk about how a TAB would benefit the whole world. Police were nightly raiding bacarrat schools in the major cities, and school children had been found betting on the Melbourne Cup.

It could be argued that the nation was doomed to hell with its gambling habits.

But, as it turned out, it was not really.

10 HIT SONGS FROM 1960:

Are You Lonesome tonight	Elvis Presley
Georgia on My Mind	Ray Charles
Polka Dot Bikini	Brian Hayland
Beyond the Sea	Bobby Darin
As Long as She Needs Me	Shirley Bassey
Wild One	Bobby Rydell
Yes Sir, She's My Baby	Johnny O'Keefe
The Twist	Chubby Checker

MOVIES RELEASED:

Never on Sunday	Melina Mercouri
Butterfield 8	Elizabeth Taylor
La Dolce Vita	Anita Eckberg
GI Blues	Elvis Presley
The Magnificent Seven	Steve McQueen
Psycho	Janet Leigh
Spartacus	Kirk Douglas
From the Terrace	Paul Newman

ACADEMY AWARDS:

Best Actor, Burt Lancaster, (Elmer Gantry)

Best Actress, Elizabeth Taylor, (Butterfield 8)

DECEMBER: CHRISTMAS - AGAIN

Well, it's back again. Whether we like it or not, Christmas keeps turning up again, and quite often, about this time of year. Dads across the nation wake up on Christmas morning with a hangover, and then sit through the agonies of present-openings, and then through two feasts and two booze-ups. But they keep coming back for more. Mums spend three days beforehand tidying up the dog hairs off the lounge, and getting those horrible venetians to slide, then put in six hours of hell cooking chooks and making jelly trifles. But they too are bent on more self destruction. As for the kids, they rip the paper off their presents, ignore all those wonderful educational books and things that are good for them, and then the boys scream about playing with guns and fighter planes and anything that has connotations of violence. The girls are now getting too sophisticated for dolls, but they like cuddly toys and cowgirl suits, with just a few bits of cosmetics.

Overall, it's a time of debauchery and gluttony, slavery, and primordial hedonism that makes us proud to acclaim our land as predominantly Christian, and at the same time satisfies our never-ending craving for the tranquillity and happiness that often comes with big family occasions.

But in case you get the feeling that the material aspects were all that mattered, I enclose the following letter, typical of many, that were printed at this time of year. Many of them were short memos that affirmed all the good aspects of Christian religions and of the celebrations, but this one below had a wider message that makes it interesting.

Letters, Warick Lindsey.   Recent arguments between two leading clergymen over matters of dogma might confuse we poor laymen. Which of the two apparently contradictory arguments is correct? The fact that such arguments could arise after 2,000 years of study makes us ask, just how solid is the ground upon which our Church is erected?

Fortunately a most encouraging answer can be found. Our Church is not erected upon the shifting ground of theology but upon a Person, the greatest thinker of all times, who shunned the doctrinaire approach, who never took the narrow or exclusive view, but whose every recorded action and mood teaches us to be tolerant.

A study of Christ, not Christianity, must surely teach us the futility of arguing dogmatically over fine points of theology. By all means let us discuss our divergent views, but never let us close our minds to the possibility that we are wrong, that other interpretations are possible. The authority of Holy Scripture can let you down badly when it has to be translated by scholars who are themselves in disagreement.

Christianity is a universal religion and affects different men in different ways, varying with their personalities and circumstances. The important thing is not to be distracted by the differences exhibited by various Christians but to be strengthened and amazed to realise that they are probably all correct, that Christianity cannot be limited by the understanding of any one person or sect, but is rather the sum total of the understanding of all who earnestly seek to be Christian.

GRAEME THORNE INQUEST

By now, accused killer Bradley was back in Australia. The inquest into the causes of Graeme's death was conduced over two weeks, and more than fifty witnesses were called. Police gave remarkable evidence of their thoroughness in pursuing the killer. For example, they took fragments of plants from the blanket that wrapped his body, and then did a house-to-house search on foot of the Dee Wye, looking for any property that was growing these two plants. They did the same with particles of soil. By such efforts they were gradually able to home in on Bradley, and with other evidence, including some witness, who identified Bradley, they were able o make the arrest.

During the inquest, a statement alleged to have been **written by Bradle**y, was submitted to the Court. The text of it read:

CONFESSION Dec 6. I have red in the newspaper that Mr Thorne won the first prise in the Operahouse Lottery. I decided that I would kidnap his son, I knew ther address from the newspaper, and I have got their phone numbr from the telephone exchange.

I went to the house to see them, I have asked for someone but cannot remembr what name. Mrs Thorne said she did not know that name and she told me to enquier in the flat upstairs.

I went upstairs and I seen the woman there. I have done this because I thoht that the Thornes will check up. I went out and wached the Thorne boy leaving the house and seen him for about three mornings and I have seen where he went and one morning I have followed him to the school at Bellevue Hill.

I parked the car in a street, I don't know the name of the street it is off Wellington Street, I have got out from the car and I waited on the conor until the boy walked down to the car. I have told the boy that I am to take him to the school. He sed why, where is the lady. I sed she is sick and cannot come today.

Then the boy got in the car and I drove him around for a while and over the harbour bridge. I went to a public phone box near the spit bridge and I rang the Thornes.

I talked to Mrs Thorne and to a man who sed he was the boys father. I have asked for 25,000 Pounds from the boys mother and father. I told them that if I don't get the money I feed him to the sharks and I have told them I ring later.

I took the boy in the car home to Clontarf and I put the car in my garage. I told the boy to get out of the car to come and see another boy. Whenn he got out of the car I have put a scarf over his mouth, and put him in the boot of the car and slammed the boot. I went in my house and the Furniture Removalist came, a few minutes after.

When it was nearly dark, I went to the car and found the boy was dead. That night I tied the boy up with string and put him in my rug.

I put the boy in the boot of the Ford Car again, and then I throw his case and cap near Bantry Bay, and I put the boy on a vacant lotment near the house I went to see with a astate agent, to buy it sometome before.

As a result of the inquest, Bradley was sent for trial for murder at a time and place to be fixed in the New Year.

IRON EXPORTS OK AGAIN

Back in 1938, the Australian government was getting uneasy because iron ore from Western Australia was being shipped to Japan and "will be sent back as bombs", as critics said. So they placed a complete embargo on the export of iron ore to Japan.

In 1960, they removed this embargo, after 22 years. This began the massive exploitation of ore that has grown ever since, to the point where it is now (in 2020) one of this nation's greatest exports.

MOTELS ON THE INCREASE

The *Sydney Morning Herald* ran a feature article that advised that the number of **motels** was growing at a rapid rate here, and that they might well be here to stay. It pointed out that there were 117 motels now in Australia, and that NSW had a total of 70, "and applications for registrations are coming every week." Officials state that Australia might eventually get to a total of 2,000 motels.

ATOMIC ESCAPE ROAD

The NSW Director of Civil Defence said that his Department was well under way in planning an escape road from Wollongong directly to the Blue Mountains in the event of an atomic attack on coastal sites. The road would not use existing roads, and would start at Warragamba Dam, and wind through virgin bush for some distance. It would be made easier by widening existing fire trails.

No such road was ever built. No atom bomb was dropped. The planning went on for decades.

SAFETY BELTS HERE?

The *SMH* ran a feature article with the headline "More NSW motorists are now using seat belts." The article points out that almost one per cent of cars were now using them and that, for example, the NSW Electricity Commission had recently ordered 50 belts on a trial basis.

The article did a world-wide survey of belt usage, and talked about the inroads the belts were making. But nowhere was there any suggestion that they would ever become mandatory. They were simply a novelty that a few safety-conscious eccentrics indulged themselves with.

NO TO THREE WEEKS LEAVE

The Australian Arbitration Commission rejected an application, from eight metal trades unions, that requested that annual leave be increased from two to three weeks. The Tribunal acknowledged the miners had recently been granted such, but said their case was special because of the time they spent underground. The judges said that, with the uncertain economy, now was not the time to take such a radical step.

CRICKET EXCITEMENT

At the First Test in Brisbane, all of the luminaries that I mentioned earlier were ready to do battle. West Indies batted first, and lived up to expectations with a rollicking 453 on a "golden day of golden cricket", with Gary Sobers adding 132. Norm O'Neill (181) and Bobby Simpson (92) took their own share of glory, and Australia edged ahead with 505 in reply.

The Indies were out for under 300 in the Second Innings, so Australia was in a fairly good position. They needed 233 runs to win, in 310 minutes, and probably could get them.

After an early collapse (5-57), Davidson and Benaud put on a partnership of 134, but another couple of wickets fell, and by the time the last (8-ball) over started, the Aussies were 7-227.

Now, if they got another six runs without getting out, they would win. If they got only four runs, they would lose. Well, what do you think they got?

Of course, you can now guess the answer. They got to 232, and lost their last wicket at the same time, **thereby ending the first tied test in history**.

Everyone was pretty pleased that such a great match had ended on this note of high excitement. The players on both sides have all become legends. Everyone of them will always be described by "**he played in the tied Test**."

The series went on for five Tests, and this was a truly splendid Series.

A THOUGHT ABOUT SPENDING

Letters, Chas Hopkins. We need to curb the current spending spree that is spreading across the nation. Some say we need bank restrictions, others say shackles on hire purchase, still others say more and more taxes on everything.

All of this while the gramophone record buying orgy goes on its merry way unchecked. Sap-brained teenagers spend millions yearly on high-priced imported discs of undiluted tripe. The noisier the record, the better it sells.

PRINCE CHARLES

London's *Daily Express* noted this morning that Prince Charles shot his first pheasants in the rain-soaked Kentish fields at Mersham. His father, the Duke of Edinburgh, was there to mentor and assist him. He was dressed in a wind-cheater coat, and boots, and had with him his own gundog, called Flash. Beaters accompanied the shooting party to flush out the pheasants. Although the rain was heavy, the young lad did not seem to mind it at all. They shot until dusk.

Letters, M de M Youngman. It was with dismay that I read that Prince Charles had shot his first pheasants. The report goes on to say that, with his father, he brought down more than a score.

Although an admirer of the British Royal Family and what it stands for, I fail to understand how its members can enjoy partaking in a "sport" of this kind, involving as it does the wilful destruction of God's defenceless creatures.

ANNOYING NOISES

Letters, D Feathestonehaugh. With other friends I recently spent a delightful weekend at Leura. We travelled by train and enjoyed comfortable carriages and adequate heating, but oh, on the return journey the horror of two transistor radios, one belonging to a lad of about 11, and at the other end of the carriage – I blush to admit it – a second in the possession of a woman old enough to know better.

Each was on a different wavelength and blaring madly. I saw someone ask her to tone it down but an indignant look was her only response. I reached Sydney with a splitting headache, and vowed "never again."

BANDICOOTS AT LAST

Now for the three letters you have waited so patiently for. We all realise that no book on Australia would be complete without bandicoot and flea coverage, and because correspondence on these flourished in the Christmas–New Year period, I had no trouble finding good samples.

Letters, Clive Firth. For over a year now, I have been waging a campaign for some official action in dealing with this problem, and as a result of his efforts the Chief Secretary has recently announced an open season until March 31 for the destruction of bandicoots on private property throughout Barrenjoey peninsula.

While this is a very welcome decision, it does not go far enough. Throughout this area, there are many large bushland reserves used for picnicking and other recreational purposes which have now become so tick-infested that it has become a very great danger to visit them. They provide the greatest portion of shelter for bandicoots.

During last Easter holiday period, our local chemist stated that over 200 people, mostly children, called on him in one week for treatment from tick-poisoning. Several were so seriously ill that he had to send them for urgent medical attention. Surely, this calls for some official action in ridding one of Sydney's most favoured recreational areas, and certainly one of the world's picked beauty spots, of such a menace. Perhaps Warringah Shire council will take the matter up. They certainly have an obligation to do so.

Letters, B Morriss. Why this agitation about ticks? The simple fact is that, if everyone spent five minutes searching their pets each day, there would be no cases of tick poisoning. If people care too little for their pets, or are too lazy, to do this, why should the bandicoots suffer? (They are among our few native animals not yet exterminated).

There is no need for the panic which seems to set in because a tick has become attached; the effects are no different in the early stages from the bite or sting of any other pests which only cause irritation. The whole matter can be easily coped with by parents or pet owners, with the help of tweezers and a little commonsense.

Disquiet is felt about the methods to be used during the open season on bandicoots. When people are given carte blanche to kill things, they use some strange and dangerous ways, in a very thoughtless manner. Many birds will die, and also quite a few of the pets which the ruling is supposed to save.

Letters, H Ellen. Many years ago, when the hinterland of Curl Curl beach was almost primitive, three friends and I occupied a small weekend shack in a clearing walled around by tea-tree. When we were eating out of doors in the dusk, we were frequently visited by a bandicoot that prowled about unobtrusively in the hope of collecting crumbs from the poor man's table.

Although we frequently pushed our way through the thick scrub of tea-tree, we neither saw nor felt a tick during our two or three years of weekend occupation. Can it be that the bandicoot performs the role of a lightning conductor, so to speak, and that it is when, owing to the inroads of settlement, the supply of bandicoots becomes insufficient to meet the needs of the tick population, that the hungry ticks turn their attention to the invading humans and their pets as their main source of sustenance?

SUMMING UP 1960

So now, 1960 has come and gone. It has been an exciting year. If you look back over these pages you will see we have covered dozens and dozens of topics, and I can assure you there were still more that I could not fit in. At the end of the year, when you compare it to other parts of the world, the nation is still prosperous and happy. Its people are free, confident and outspoken, and ready for anything.

If you look closely, you will find things that need fixing, and some of these will get attention in the next decade. Aborigines and women and working conditions will get their fair share. As it will turn out, our economy will not stay as buoyant as it is now, and all those festering points of conflict round the world will not go away.

But to go back to the world view, what a lucky country we are at 1960. By 1964, Donald Horne had written his famous book, of that title, telling of the philistinism, provincialism, and dependence in the nation and saying we were mired in mediocrity and manacled to the past. He was completely right in all that, but when you look at the rest of the world, we were still so lucky. In fact, my opinion is that we were not the lucky country, but instead, the luckiest country. Remember the atomic submarine base in Britain nestling in a small sea-side town, remember the riots in South Africa, and the conflicts in the Congo and Algeria, and remember the poverty of dozens of nations, and get some perspective.

We were a million miles away from all these atrocities and we were somehow very prosperous. If the price we had to pay was that we were a bit backward by someone's standards, then so be it.

So, I suggest you do not pack up and leave this nation, but rather stick it out for another 50 or 100 years. I can promise you, with my clear vision of the future, that for most people most of the time, things will get even better.